Virtue Ethics

Ethics Study Guide

Peter Baron

First published 2014

by PushMe Press

Mid Somerset House, Southover, Wells, Somerset BA5 1UH

www.pushmepress.com

© 2014 Inducit Learning Ltd

The right of Peter Baron to be identified as author of this work has been asserted by him in accordance with sections 77 and 78 of the Copyright, Designs and Patents Act 1988.

All rights reserved. No part of this book may be reprinted or reproduced or utilised in any form or transmitted by any electronic, mechanical, or other means, now known or hereafter invented, including photocopying and recording, or in any information storage or retrieval system, without permission in writing from the publishers.

British Library Cataloguing in Publication Data
A catalogue record for this book is available from the British Library

ISBN: 978-1-909618-24-4 (pbk)
ISBN: 978-1-909618-25-1 (ebk)
ISBN: 978-1-78484-018-1 (hbk)
ISBN: 978-1-78484-019-8 (pdf)

Typeset in Frutiger by booksellerate.com
Printed by Lightning Source

Contents

Introduction..1
Aristotelian Virtue Ethics..7
MacIntyre's Virtue Ethics..29
Philippa Foot's Virtue Ethics....................................45
Christian Virtue Ethics 53
Applied Virtue Ethics 71
Evaluating Virtue Ethics 87
The Four Questions Revisited 97
Key Quotes 105

Introduction

THE NATURE OF VIRTUE ETHICS

Virtue Ethics is the ethics of character and character formation and, for this reason, is sometimes described as "agent-centred" to contrast it with rule-based ethical theories. The agent here is the person who is choosing to pursue some end and doing so for good reasons. So a virtue is usually defined as either a disposition of character or an inclination of character - the first definition highlighting the habitual nature of the virtues, and the second, the link between virtue and will.

A disposition implies a tendency of an individual to behave in a certain way. I am disposed to be merciful, we say. The disposition means that I both feel merciful (emotion) and by habit act mercifully (nature). It is, in other words, about my feelings and my second nature. The word inclination suggests I actually want to be merciful and take pleasure in acts of mercy. This is important because some moral theories play down feelings (Kantian ethics) and others play down intention and will (utilitarian ethics). Virtue ethics stresses both. We should be disposed to be virtuous but also enjoy being virtuous.

And there is a third element of virtue ethics contained in the very Greek word **ARETE**. Arete (literally, virtue) means skill or excellence in this context. The idea of skill implies a habit of reason - something we learn by practice until it becomes (the phrase I introduced above) second nature. These three elements - will, emotion and reasoned practice - give us a clue as to why virtue ethics has assumed such popularity amongst ethical theories in the 20th C - it seems to involve the whole human being, mind, spirit and will.

Virtue ethics has its origin in ancient Greek ethics and is closely aligned in Greek thought with Natural Law. This means that virtue ethics arises from the Greek teleological worldview where everything including human beings, has a purpose. Whether or not we accept virtue ethics as the defining moral theory will depend, however, on our answer to a number of questions, and whether we find the answers plausible. These four questions spell the acronym **DARM**, and I return to answer them in detail in a final chapter.

1. **DERIVATION** - Where do the virtues come from? Presuppositions define the origins of every ethical theory, and virtue ethics is no exception. To a Kantian, ethics comes from autonomous reason, and values of good and bad arise out of a universalising reasoning process. The key assumption is autonomy - we must be free to reason. To a utilitarian, ethical norms arise out of a calculation of consequences after we have accepted that happiness or pleasure is the only intrinsic good. But to the virtue ethicist, norms can arise either out of a set of metaphysical assumptions (where metaphysical means "beyond physics" or essentially unprovable) or out of an observation about how groups work. We need to examine the assumptions of virtue ethics and test their validity. We can also ask what is the social context of the virtues? Virtue, be it a classical Greek or a modern conception of virtue, always has a social dimension. In other words, it is about how the individual relates to others within society or within a sub-group. But how does this social dimension relate to individual choice?

2. **APPLICATION** - How do we apply the virtues? A virtue is a character trait - something we observe in human behaviour. To take an example: if the virtue of honesty is accepted as "good", in what situations do we need honesty? And exactly what does

honesty mean? Kant, for example, got into trouble for arguing that there was a categorical imperative never to lie - but to a virtue ethicist, being honest doesn't necessarily include always telling the exact truth. But how do we decide what form of honesty to employ in any given situation? How do we decide when to be "brutally honest", "diplomatically guarded" and when to employ deliberate deception?

3. **REALISM** - Elisabeth Anscombe (1958) argued that moral philosophies lack an adequate philosophy of moral psychology (see below). She seemed to imply by this that ethical theories lacked realism when it came to practical living - that they belong to a now defunct worldview where, for example, God was seen as the giver of law and we were supposed, as willing subjects, to obey. Is there something about the virtue ethical worldview which has a more realistic appreciation of how human psychology works?

4. **MOTIVATION** - Virtue ethicists criticise other theories such as Kantian ethics and utilitarianism for failing to provide an adequate answer to the question "why should I be moral?". Rosalind Hursthouse, for example, criticises Kant for failing to explain how we achieve "the strength of will or systematic reorientation of emotions such that you standardly treat people as having human dignity, with the right light in your eye". (2006:163) Kant has difficulty doing this because he argues that emotions are irrelevant to the moral decision or that emotions get in the way of a pure idea of rationality. Can virtue ethics do better?

In this book we compare three virtue ethicists and their answers to these three questions. We begin our analysis with Aristotelian virtue ethics before comparing that with the virtue ethics of Alasdair MacIntyre in the modern era, as expressed in his early work, After Virtue. We then consider a third modern virtue ethicist, Philippa Foot, by examining her last book, Natural Goodness. To what extent can either of these be termed "Aristotelian?", meaning to what extent do they provide a modern update of Aristotle, and where do they depart radically from his analysis of the virtues?.

We then consider the nature of Christian virtue ethics and analyse a recent book, Virtue Reborn, by Tom Wright, former Bishop of Durham. Can we describe Jesus as an ancient virtue ethicist? In what ways does Christian Virtue Ethics differ from more secular approaches?

This will be a selective survey. We could have taken any number of virtue ethicists, for example Robert Louden, Rosalind Hursthouse (whose views will in fact be used to illustrate the applied ethics of abortion and the environment in chapter 6, or Michael Slote. But in focusing on these four writers, ancient and modern, we can draw out the essential features of virtue ethics and ultimately evaluate whether virtue ethics is a workable solution to Socrates' ancient question, "how then should I live?"

ELIZABETH ANSCOMBE

In 1958 Elizabeth Anscombe wrote a short article in the journal Philosophy in which she argued that ethics had reached a dead end in following a law-based path when the original law-giver (God) had all but been abandoned. She begins with three bold claims:

> *I will begin by stating three theses which I present in this paper. The first is that it is not profitable for us at present to do moral philosophy; that should be laid aside until we have an adequate philosophy of psychology, in which we are conspicuously lacking. The second is that the concepts of obligation and duty ought to be jettisoned if this is psychologically possible; because they are survivals, from an earlier conception of ethics which no longer generally survives, and are only harmful without it. My third thesis is that the differences between the well-known English writers on moral philosophy are of little importance.*

Anscombe appeals to us to find a new naturalism which will explain why we are obliged to do something - to ground our idea of what we ought to do. This new **NATURALISM** will have its grounding in a theory of human nature, of what makes human beings think and feel and understand their own welfare. The "norm", or values we derive from human nature, will be integrated with an agreed understanding of what it means to flourish. In other words, it will be grounded in an understanding of what features of our shared lives help us to grow and develop and realise our true potential. Moral obligation comes out of a different concept of "norm", one closer to the idea of "what is normal for a human being". She writes:

> "Man" with the complete set of virtues is the "norm", as "man" with, for example, a complete set of teeth is a norm. But in this sense 'norm' has ceased to be roughly equivalent to "law". In this sense the notion of a "norm" brings us nearer to an Aristotelian than a law conception of ethics.

The new concept of ethics she is describing has its origin in character and character formation towards a specific end - the flourishing life. In this sense it is nearer to Aristotle's idea of goodness. It is far away from the idea of norm to the Kantian, who stresses the moral law as a set of **CATEGORICALS** in a deontological duty-based ethic, or utilitarianism, which asks us to calculate consequences but has no reference to motive or social setting and so is, for Anscombe, a "shallow theory". She concludes:

> It can be seen that philosophically there is a huge gap, at present unfillable as far as we are concerned, which needs to be filled by an account of human nature, human action, the type of characteristic a virtue is, and above all of human "flourishing".

This then, is the challenge she laid down, and we will examine how the virtue ethics of the classical and the modern period attempt to meet this challenge and to what extent they succeed in grounding ethics in character traits and some concept of human flourishing.

Aristotelian Virtue Ethics

Aristotle was born in a small city-state called Stagirus at a time when it was usual to accept the institution of slavery and the inferiority of women. He accepted both uncritically, but nonetheless I believe his theory of virtue and its relation to society can be rescued from its cultural context to produce a compelling account of how human beings beget wisdom and virtue and hence achieve a happy, fulfilled life.

WHAT IS A VIRTUE?

Aristotle sees a virtue as a state of character which is achieved through the application of practical wisdom to the goal of living well. He begins his Nichomachean ethics by arguing that "every action and pursuit is thought to aim at some good, and for this reason the good has been declared to be that at which all things aim" (Nichomachean Ethics 1.1). What is this intrinsic good at which we all aim, our goal or telos? It is nothing less than happiness, but happiness defined in a certain sort of way. The Greek word for it is **EUDAIMONIA**.

Eudaimonia is something which is developed as a result of practising the skills of living which build a flourishing life. Or put another way, if we were to think hard about the kind of characteristics we need to develop our full potential, we would come up with certain skills which, if practised, allow us to handle the ups and downs of life and use our own natural gifts wisely.

Eudaimonia is the ultimate end which is good in itself (intrinsically good) and willed for its own sake. Aristotle calls it an "activity of the soul in accordance with virtue", with the end of living well or excellently. It includes both a personal and a social dimension. The individual requires the development of practical wisdom and knowledge in order to live well, and the political system requires justice. He writes:

> *If we consider the function of man to be a certain kind of life, and this to be an activity of the soul in accordance with reason, and the function of a good man to be the noble performance of these, and if any action is well performed when it is performed in accordance with the appropriate principle; if this is the case, human good turns out to be activity of the soul in accordance with virtue. (1926: I.7)*

Broadly, Aristotle sees two types of virtue, the intellectual and the moral. Intellectual virtues create knowledge. For example, scientific knowledge is produced by its own rational activity of experimentation. The end result of this process is an expertise or wisdom, the fruit of a good education, which Aristotle calls **SOPHIA**.

Moral knowledge is built a different way, through experience, and hence it is practical wisdom. The technical word for this is **PHRONESIS**, which is sometimes translated as prudence or practical wisdom. I prefer the meaning "right judgement." The skill of phronesis is developed by contemplation and deliberation on our mistakes and triumphs, our strengths and weaknesses, our successes and failures. So the ultimate aim is to become one skilled in practice - **PRAXIS** - as a philosopher or lover of wisdom, so that we judge in a right (appropriate) way.

In order to unpack this further and trace the relationship between the virtues and eudaimonia or happiness, we need to examine the origins of the Greek teleological worldview that places function at its heart, and to see how this explains the metaphysical basis of Aristotle's teleology.

ARISTOTLEAN METAPHYSICS

The word "meta" means beyond or behind and so **METAPHYSICS** means behind the physical world and not subject to any empirical test which we might apply to objects. The metaphysical basis of Aristotelian ethics is his idea of form and function, as in the statement "the function of a human being is a certain kind of life" in the quote opposite. The idea of form and function helps us to map the soul so that we understand the relation between the rational and the non-rational sides of the soul. Ethics then becomes the process of self-mastery, or what Aristotle calls "continence".

The Four Causes

Substances (things) have four causes which bring them from **POTENTIALITY** to **ACTUALITY**. The material cause is the stuff something is made of - the stuff human beings are made of is flesh and blood for example. The formal cause is the idea, or blueprint, of human beings, what makes us distinctively human, and the efficient cause is a mother and father mating and then nurturing a child, which is what brings the formal cause about. Lastly there is the **FINAL CAUSE**, or purpose of a human being, which Aristotle has already defined as the eudaimonic life - the life lived excellently, built by virtue, so that we flourish and attain our true potential. The eudaimonic life, to repeat, is the only thing good in itself.

The formal causes can also be seen as the form of a human being. This is something which is synonymous with the soul. The soul is the form or formal cause which makes us distinctively human, or to be exact, the soul is the potential of a human being which needs to be actualised in practice. Aristote calls this the "first actuality" - where potential exists but has to be realised by fulfilling our true function, which is the exercise of our reason.

So Aristotle uses the idea of first actuality in his definition of the soul:

> *The soul is the first actuality of a natural body that is potentially alive. (Metaphysics 412a27)*

Animals have a soul which is distinctive for animals. For example, animals grow and develop and feel hunger and require food, what Aristotle calls the nutritive part and appetitive parts of the soul. But human beings have something unique - the ability to reason and to choose. This rational and deliberative function of the soul involves both potentiality and actuality.

- **POTENTIALITY** - The potential to reason.
- **ACTUALITY** - The exercise of reason to develop practical wisdom.

So when Aristotle talks about the "function of man" he is speaking of both the potential and the actual. Function includes both reason itself as an idea and a potential, and reason as an activity of the soul. Only if human beings act on this potential and build the skill of practical wisdom through deliberation do they "actualise" their human souls. This process of disciplining the soul in the pursuit of the higher end of eudaimonia can be illustrated diagrammatically.

Rational soul	**Non rational soul**
CALCULATIVE PART	NUTRITIVE PART
Science	Growth
Maths	Self-nourishment
DELIBERATIVE PART	APPETITIVE PART
Practical wisdom (phronesis)	Food, sex, drink
	Feelings, emotions

Aristotle's idea of the soul

The intellectual virtue of phronesis controls the appetitive side by bringing right reason to bear on passions, feelings and desires, so moralising our choices and building the flourishing life.

Starting at the left-hand side, Aristotle sees the soul as a rational entity. We possess the potential to acquire knowledge through education, and practical wisdom through experience. The self-controlled person will exercise self-mastery over the appetites and desires on the right-hand side of the diagram - the non-rational side of the soul which we share with animals. How exactly does this self-mastery work? It works through the learnt skill of **PHRONESIS**, or practical wisdom. Practical wisdom helps us understand how the exercise of virtue establishes the flourishing life. This is not so much a matter of establishing hard and fast rules as exercising judgement.

PHRONESIS IS THE KEY

Phronesis is the key to soul-building. It is phronesis that allows us to make right judgements. We learn phronesis as a habit so that it becomes second nature - more like a moral instinct. But **PHRONIMOI** (wise people) are made, not born. So, unlike many Christian philosophers (Butler, Aquinas), Aristotle does not see this ability as innate (something we are born with). Rather, it is built three ways:

EDUCATION - We learn by listening to wise moral teachers who show us how to reason well when faced with moral dilemmas.

EMULATION - We learn by copying our moral heroes, those who are heroic in justice, or integrity or honesty - who handle these virtues excellently.

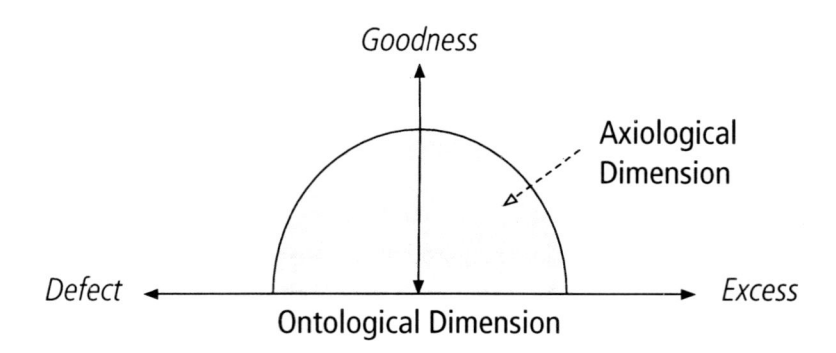

EXPERIENCE - We learn by trying to live the virtuous life. The experience has two parts to it. First, we need to know what the virtues are. We need to understand what the four classic virtues (wisdom, temperance, courage and justice), sometimes called cardinal virtues, mean. And secondly, we need to learn how to apply them in different circumstances.

In a brilliant TED lecture, Barry Schwartz lays down four implications of practical wisdom or phronesis.

1. The wise person is made, not born.
2. The wise person knows when to make an exception to the rule.
3. The wise person is like a jazz player, able to improvise as the situation demands.
4. You don't have to be intelligent to be wise. You just need the moral will and the moral skill.

So, to take up Anscombe's challenge of explaining the virtues to the modern era, the Aristotelian argues that once we have the clear goal of the flourishing life we can learn the skills of practical wisdom in identifying and then judging the appropriate virtue in the circumstances. Of course, it will depend on my own character as to which virtue makes up for something I naturally lack. Take courage for example. Some people may be naturally bold and others naturally cautious. But each individual needs to discern both the nature and appropriate application of the virtue in question.

That's how we become skilled improvisers in the game of life.

APPLYING THE VIRTUES

In order to understand how we apply the virtues in different situations we need to understand how Aristotle explains his idea of the golden mean. He writes:

> *That moral virtue is a mean, then, and in what sense it is so, and that it is a mean between two vices, the one involving excess, the other deficiency, and that it is such because its character is to aim at what is intermediate in passions and in actions, has been sufficiently stated. Hence also it is no easy task to be good. For in everything it is no easy task to find the middle, eg to find the middle of a circle is not for everyone but for him who knows; so, too, any one can get angry - that is easy - or give or spend money; but to do this to the right person, to the right extent, at the right time, with the right motive, and in the right way, that is not for every one, nor is it easy; wherefore goodness is both rare and laudable and noble. (1926: II.9)*

The philosophy.lander.edu website (a site that contains many useful resources) explains it thus: in the ontological dimension representing reality, virtue is a mean or as Aristotle describes it "an intermediate position"; in the axiological dimension representing value, it is an extreme or excellence.

Martin Luther King, Jr relates his struggle to understand this difference in his "Letter from Birmingham Jail" when he wrote,

> *You speak of our activity in Birmingham as extreme ... But though I was initially disappointed at being categorised as an extremist, as I continued to think about the matter I gradually*

gained a measure of satisfaction from the label. Was not Jesus an extremist for love? Was not Amos an extremist for justice? Was not Paul an extremist for the Christian gospel? Perhaps the South, the nation and the world are in dire need of creative extremists.

Hence "appropriate judgement" is not just about right application of the virtue, but includes right motive, right amount (extreme anger or nor very much) and right timing. The excellence that results on the value scale is extreme - the virtuous person is extremely beautiful - **KALOS** - and noble. As Martin Luther King observes, Amos was an extremist for justice and we could also say Jesus was an extremist for love. In virtue ethics, extremism often implies excellence.

A JUDGEMENT POINT BETWEEN TWO VICES

Phronesis, then, allows us to make the right judgement about the application of the virtue. We can apply this to the virtues discussed by Aristotle himself to give us some idea of the twin vices of excess and deficiency.

Sphere	Excess	Mean	Deficiency
Fear	*Rashness*	*Courage*	*Cowardice*
Pleasure	*Indulgence*	*Temperance*	*Abstinence*
Money	*Wastefulness*	*Generosity*	*Meanness*
Acquisition	*Tastelessness*	*Magnificence*	*Niggardliness*
Pride	*Vanity*	*Magnanimity*	*Self-deprecation*
Justice	*Irritability*	*Anger*	*Apathy*
Friendship	*Flattery*	*Amity*	*Surliness*
Humour	*Friviolity*	*Wittiness*	*Boorishness*

Some of these virtues may surprise us. For example, Greeks saw pride as a virtue, whereas we tend to see pride as a vice and, influenced by Christianity, humility as a virtue. But what do the Greeks mean by pride?

Pride is the ability to value yourself according to your true worth. It is to be confident in your abilities and unashamed to volunteer your skills. It is an overarching virtue, one which is the culmination of all the virtues and so best described not with the misleading English word "pride" but with the literal Greek translation of a "great-souled person".

Its contrast is the small-souled person, and Aristotle explains "most small-souled of all would seem to be the man who claims less than he deserves when his deserts are great". This seems to imply a lack of self-knowledge and a lack of self-worth. Failure to recognise and believe in your own skill and ability is clearly a vice which cannot produce a eudaimonic life.

Finally, magnificence would seem to be a strange addition. By this Aristotle really means acquiring the best which you can afford. It is this virtue that chooses the BMW over the Daewoo Matiz because (to borrow an advertising slogan) you're worth it.

THE CARDINAL VIRTUES

The four cardinal (literally "hinge") virtues of Greek ethics are wisdom, justice, temperance and courage. The idea of cardinal virtues was first defined by Thomas Aquinas, and in a final section of this chapter we will consider how Aquinas built on the Aristotelian virtues to produce a distinctively Christian take on virtue. We have already said something about wisdom (phronesis) as the highest intellectual virtue, but what of temperance and justice?

Aristotle argues that temperance is the skill of self-control without which the incontinent man will lose his way in the pursuit of unbridled pleasure. It is this virtue which seems ill at ease with the modern era. For, influenced as we are by the utilitarian emphasis on pleasure as an intrinsic good, and the pursuit of pleasure as a fundamental human right, we have difficulty saying no and delaying gratification of the senses. It is hardly surprising then that this is the age of growing addictions (alcohol, gambling, or varieties of sexual addiction for example).

Aristotle particularly emphasises bodily pleasures (the lower pleasures of Mill's utilitarian classification). Particularly, he stresses the pleasures of sensuality and of taste (food and drink). We might elaborate in our own age the exaltation of the pleasures of sex and of drink. If we are to choose wisely, according to practical wisdom, then we will desire things that build up a healthy mind and body, and practices which are beautiful not ugly. And beauty here implies no exploitation of the other person, to use the Kantian formula, not treating others as a means to our own selfish end.

The cardinal virtue of justice, in contrast, is the key to building the political life. Remember that the state of **EUDAIMONIA,** or human flourishing, exists in two dimensions, the personal and the social. So justice will be crucial in building a virtuous (excellent) city-state, or polis. To Aristotle, the state must come first because, without a state guaranteeing justice, the individual cannot flourish. In his own words, Aristotle argues that the social instinct is something natural to humankind, and law and justice the glue that holds a society together.

> *A social instinct is implanted in all men by nature, and yet he who first founded the state was the greatest of benefactors. For man, when perfected, is the best of animals, but, when separated from law and justice, he is the worst of all; since armed injustice is the more dangerous, and he is equipped at birth with arms, meant to be used by intelligence and virtue, which he may use for the worst ends. Wherefore, if he have not virtue, he is the most unholy and the most savage of animals, and the most full of lust and gluttony. But justice is the bond of men in states, for the administration of justice, which is the determination of what is just, is the principle of order in political society. (Politics, Book I part ii)*

Justice, or fairness, then, is the social virtue that gives everyone what is their right or their desert and arbitrates when tensions and disputes arise. John Hardon defines justice as "the constant and permanent determination to give everyone his or her rightful due". The distinctiveness of the virtue of justice has three elements:

JUSTICE IS POSITIVE - It is about building a fair society where we respect one another, and also recognise that the rights of others limit one's own behaviour. For example, the right of free speech entails the duty to listen and not to abuse; the right of property entails the duty not to steal. Justice is not only about fair retribution for crimes committed, it is also about fair distribution of rights and benefits.

JUSTICE IS BOTH A NATURAL RIGHT AND A LEGAL RIGHT - We all possess natural rights by virtue of being human. As the American Declaration of Independence puts it:

> *We hold these truths to be self-evident, that all men are created equal, that they are endowed by their Creator with certain unalienable Rights, that among these are Life, Liberty, and the Pursuit of Happiness. That to secure these rights, Governments are instituted among Men, deriving their just powers from the consent of the governed.*

But legal rights and natural rights may conflict. For example, Aristotle sees the family as the natural focus for justice and law - the origin of social rules. But if I fail in my right and duty to educate my children and ensure they go to school my right to supervise my child can be taken away - we hear of children being taken into care of a local authority. In this way the laws of society may choose to limit my natural rights.

JUSTICE CIVILISES THE DESIRE FOR REVENGE - Francis Bacon observed that "Revenge is a kind of wild justice, which the more man's nature runs to, the more ought law to weed out; for the first wrong, it doth offend the law, but the revenge of that wrong, putteth the law out of office." We all have an instinctive sense that retribution is required in order to right past wrongs - that the criminal deserves a punishment appropriate to the crime. But how to civilise this sense? The answer in Greek ethics was to ground the operation of justice in the city-state through rules and the operation of a legal process. Defendants could be tried but also defended by an advocate. The Greeks first invented the jury system and the presiding judge. In this way we have, in Greek virtue ethics, the foundations of our modern system of justice. Revenge must be mediated by the state and a transparent process of judgement by our peers.

Michael Sandel of Harvard University sums up the Aristotelian view this way:

> *Aristotle believes that justice consists in giving people what they deserve, and that a just society is one that enables human beings to realise their highest nature and to live the good life. For Aristotle, political activity is not merely a way to pursue our interests, but an essential part of the good life.*

THE ISSUE OF NATURAL CLASSES

Having praised Greek virtue ethics for founding our system of justice, we need to mark an objection to the natural law/virtue ethics tradition which was movingly portrayed by the 2014 film 12 Years a Slave. The objection is that Aristotle saw nothing unjust in the division of society by strata with unequal rights: slave and free person, male and female. These elements of the body politic are by nature unequal, argues Aristotle in the Politics:

> *But is there anyone thus intended by nature to be a slave, and for whom such a condition is expedient and right, or rather is not all slavery a violation of nature? There is no difficulty in answering this question, on grounds both of reason and of fact. For that some should rule and others be ruled is a thing not only necessary, but expedient; from the hour of their birth, some are marked out for subjection, others for rule. (Politics I, book iii)*

Aristotle argues that the relation of master to slave and male to female is as natural to the social order as the relation of body to soul is in the constitution of a human being. Recall how, in the constitution of the soul, the rational part of the soul needs to bring into subjection unruly appetites and passions and that the key virtue to regulate the unruly soul is phronesis. In the same way, argues Aristotle, in the polis or city-state the wise rulers (philosophers) need to bring those who are by nature unruly (slaves and women) under control for the common good. He concedes that there is an issue here, for some argue that this violates the natural equality of all human beings.

> *And it is clear that the rule of the soul over the body, and of the mind and the rational element over the passionate, is natural and expedient; whereas the equality of the two or the rule of the inferior is always hurtful. The same holds good of animals in relation to men; for tame animals have a better nature than wild, and all tame animals are better off when they are ruled by man; for then they are preserved. Again, the male is by nature superior, and the female inferior; and the one rules, and the*

other is ruled; this principle, of necessity, extends to all mankind. (Politics Book I part V)

Aristotle does make one concession to our modern view. He argues that lordship must be of a certain sort because both master and slave belong to the one body politic, just as body and soul belong to the one human being. So if the master abuses the slave then the body as a whole will suffer. The master must still relate to the slave in a manner consistent with the virtues, even if the slave is by nature seen to be inferior.

In 12 Years a Slave we find echoes of this ancient Greek debate. Epps, the evil slave master who abuses his slave "property", quotes Scripture in arguing for the natural state of slavery. But when Bass (played by Brad Pitt) challenges his view, he appeals to a natural law argument.

Bass: The law says you have the right to hold a black man, but begging the law's pardon, it lies. Is everything right because the law allows it? Suppose they'd pass a law taking away your liberty and making you a slave?

Edwin Epps: Ha!

Bass: Suppose!

Edwin Epps: That ain't a supposable case.

Bass: Because the law states that your liberties are undeniable? Because society deems it so? Laws change. Social systems crumble. Universal truths are constant. It is a fact, it is a plain fact that what is true and right is true and right for all. White and black alike.

Aristotle seems to reject this view that there is a universal truth that all men are born equal, and this suggests a weakness in the application of virtue. The weakness lies in Aristotle's metaphysical view of natural states - for just as we may reject his idea of the soul as split between different rational and irrational elements, so we recoil from and reject the view which holds that the soul of the body politic is also split between slave and free, male and female, with the one naturally superior to the other.

AQUINAS'S ACCOUNT OF THE VIRTUES

Aquinas shares with Aristotle the view that the exercise of virtue is about creating habits which we practise, which are natural to our species as human beings. In a general sense, a virtue is a habit that "disposes an agent to perform its proper operation or movement" (Summa Theologica Ia, IIae 49.1). The function that makes us human is reason, and the key to excellence of character is to reason well. Building virtue is therefore a rational activity of the soul - practising that key virtue of phronesis or practical wisdom.

Aquinas argues that there is a special relation between the will, our choice of an end, and our reason. Just as Aristotle divides the soul between intellectual reason and unruly appetite, so Aquinas argues it is the intellect which determines what is good about some end we pursue. The intellect needs to rule over our appetites according to our rational assessment of the goodness of the end.

> *As the intellect of necessity adheres to first principles, the will must of necessity adhere to the last end, which is happiness. (Summa Theologica Ia 82.1)*

So according to Aquinas the intellect and will are related in this way - the intellect understands the first principles of our natural state (the primary precepts of natural law theory). The intellect grasps universal truth. But we then need what Aquinas calls the appetitive power of reason - the will to choose that end. The will follows the directions of the intellect. The objective we are aiming for moves the will as a final cause or end, but the objective itself is determined by a process of reason.

Here we come to the first modification of Aristotle's teleology. Remember that Aristotle sees the final end as eudaimonia - the fulfilment of the individual in a life which integrates the virtues to realise our true potential. But to Aquinas, this ultimate end is only relayed by our perfection in heaven. He argues:

> *Everyone desires the fulfillment of their perfection, and it is precisely this fulfilment in which the final end consists. (Summa Theologica Ia, IIae 1.7)*

MacDonald explains this idea of perfection as a "formal concept ... of the complete and perfect good, that which completely satisfies desire" (MacDonald, 1991: 61). But how is this happiness or perfection realised? Only by God and in God, in the state of blessedness (beatitude) which we call heaven. God fulfils us in the deepest sense, as Augustine observed, "We are made towards God and our hearts are restless until they find their rest in Him."

To achieve this end we will need faith and the gift of grace. Without those things we are liable to make mistakes, to pursue the wrong things - we can make a mistake of reasoning or the passions and appetites (Aristotelian echoes again) can lead us away from the path of virtue. For this reason we need to want, desire, long for the virtues which will make us beautiful.

NATURAL AND INFUSED VIRTUE

So far we have seen that Aquinas takes the Aristotelian idea of eudaimonia (human flourishing) and enriches it with the idea of heavenly blessedness. Our true fulfilment as human beings is only possible in the state of grace. This is because the struggle is too great by ourselves: we need the help of God the Holy Spirit to establish the virtues as second nature.

It is Aquinas who first identifies four cardinal virtues which are implicit in Greek ethics: prudence (**PRUDENTIA** in Latin, **PHRONESIS** in Greek), justice, courage and temperance. But he also argues that they are not enough by themselves to achieve blessedness. We need to achieve a "happiness that surpasses human nature", and for this we will need God's help. He writes:

> *Man is perfected by virtue, for by those actions he is directed to happiness. Now man's happiness is twofold. One comes from our human nature, a happiness which we obtain by natural principles. The other is a happiness surpassing man's nature, and which we can obtain by the power of God alone, by a kind of participation in the Godhead, about which it is written (2 Peter 1:4) that by Christ we are made "partakers of the Divine nature". Such happiness surpasses the capacity of human nature. Hence it is necessary for man to receive from God some additional principles, whereby he may be directed to supernatural happiness, called "theological virtues": First, because their focus is God, as they direct us aright to God; secondly, because they are infused in us by God alone; thirdly, because these virtues are not made known to us, save by Divine*

> *revelation in the Bible. (Summa ·Theologica Ia, IIae 61.2, abridged)*

What are these virtues which are infused or poured into us by the Holy Spirit? They are no less than the virtues Paul lists in 1 Corinthians 13, the virtues of faith, hope and love. Where our natural reason directs towards the four cardinal virtues, with the universal aim of eudaimonia or happiness, the theological virtues direct us to God himself, and their end is eternal blessedness, the happy state of being with God forever in heaven. As Paul reminds us, "the greatest of these is love" (1 Corinthians 13:13). The divine end is given us by the gift of faith; the ability of our wills to keep on going by the gift of hope, and the motivation to act on what God wills is given to us by the gift of love. So love is the greatest virtue of all.

THE GREATEST OF ALL IS LOVE

To the unredeemed non-Christian soul, the greatest virtue of all is phronesis or practical wisdom, as without this we will never make the appropriate judgements that build the flourishing life. But to the redeemed soul that receives grace, the gift of God, the greatest virtue of all is love. What then is this virtue and how does it operate?

Aquinas argues that charity, love, precedes faith and hope and is the "form of them all".

> *But in the order of perfection, charity precedes faith and hope, because both faith and hope are brought alive by charity, and receive from charity their full complement as virtues. For thus*

> charity is the mother and the root of all the virtues, inasmuch as it is the form of them all. (Summa Theologica Ia, IIae, 62).

It is by the infused virtue of love that the Holy Spirit creates in us both the desire and the power to do loving acts. The Holy Spirit remoulds our wills so that we take pleasure in loving. But, Aquinas stresses, it has to be our wills that do the loving, inspired and empowered by God, because love that is forced would no longer be love. He concludes:

> For us to perform the act of charity, there should be in us some habitual form added to the natural power, inclining that power to the act of charity, and causing it to act with ease and pleasure.

Love then is the supreme infused virtue. It unites us to God, it stems from the very essence of God (God is love) and it is our motivator to put into effect all the other virtues. We tread the path of love, and to do so is to tread a path of ease and pleasure, as, inspired by God the Holy Spirit, we grow into perfection, and in the end dwell eternally in perfect unity with God in heaven.

MacIntyre's Virtue Ethics

In recent years the reinterpretation of virtue ethics has involved, at least partially, the rehabilitation of Aristotle as one of the original Greek sources of a theory of character formation as a guide to practical action, which is what we understand by "virtue ethics". In this chapter I consider the similarities and differences between MacIntyre's account of the virtues as expressed in After Virtue (AV) and Aristotle's in Nichomachean Ethics (NE), and ask the question whether the two accounts can be reconciled. (It is important to limit this analysis to After Virtue because in later works MacIntyre changed his mind about the place of metaphysics in his scheme.)

MacIntyre, while accepting Aristotle's account of practical reason - **PHRONESIS** - and its role in guiding actions, explicitly rejects three elements of Aristotle's scheme of thought: his metaphysical biology; his belief in the centrality of the polis or city-state in the formation of virtues; and his explanation of the **GOLDEN MEAN** as a way of applying the virtues in a way that arguably may be said to fit human psychology.

The essential contrast between MacIntyre and Aristotle is summarised in the table below. Here I will concentrate on the origin of the good, considering how Aristotle's metaphysics performs against MacIntyre's sociology, and the psychology inherent in the idea of the Golden Mean.

Virtues	MacIntyre	Aristotle
Origin	Social	Biological
Comment - MacIntyre disagrees with Aristotle's metaphysical biology. He argues for the centrality of social practices		
Source	Practices	Human Nature
Comment - Aristotle assumes one human nature. MacIntyre sees a plurality of practices		
Process	Narrative structure	Personal Judgement
Comment - We learn the virtues by pursuing our own story embedded in communities we share. Aristotle sees virtues as a golden mean or judgement point		
End	Social excellence	Happiness / flourishing life
Comment - MacIntyre argues we pursue the unity of a narrative quest. Aristotle sees human flourishing deriving from who we are		
Teleology	Fixed by human tradition	Fixed by human essence
Comment - Our goals are set by the tradition of the practices we inhabit. To Aristotle, the goal is given by a shared understanding of flourishing.		
Form of society	Egalitarian	Elitist
Comment - Aristotle favours aristocracy, slavery and subordination of women. MacIntyre is closer to Marxism		
Internal goods	Internal to practices	Internal to the psyche
Comment - Both distinguish between intrinsic good (internal) and instrumental (external), but defined in different ways		
Traditions	Pluralistic	Aristocratic
Comment - Aristotle argues for a natural order of society. MacIntyre is against institutions which suppress virtue.		

WORLDVIEWS

Aristotle was lecturing in 346 BC, in an era of pre-modernity, whereas After Virtue, written in 1971, expresses the assumptions of a postmodern mind. Aristotle sees the world as a unified whole, with relationships between physics and metaphysics, and with all the virtues uniting to achieve one common human purpose or **TELOS**, that of **EUDAIMONIA**. This overall purpose is the only thing that is good in itself, argues Aristotle, and the goodness lies in the excellence which a life of virtue will bring. So eudaimonia is best seen as personal and social flourishing, where the virtuous citizen participates in goals and activities that build the social good. Aristotle's definition of virtue is essentially different from MacIntyre's because of this holistic assumption:

> *The Good of man is the active exercise of his soul in conformity with excellence or virtue, or if there be several human excellences or virtues, in conformity with the best and most perfect among them. Moreover, to be happy takes a complete lifetime; for one swallow does not make a spring. (1926:I. 7.1098a)*

Notice that Aristotle stresses the soul or **PSYCHE**. The activity of the soul is to bring the appetites and desires under the rational control of the will. We have to conform to virtue or excellence by making active choices to prevent irrational passions and desires leading us astray into bad actions. This is the first element of what MacIntyre calls Aristotle's "metaphysical biology".

The second element is an assumption Aristotle makes. (Stanley Hauweras quotes MacIntyre's revised emphasis on metaphysics. "It is only because human beings have an end toward which they are directed by reason of their specific nature that practices, traditions, and the like are able to function as they do.") There is one fixed human nature which results from our **FINAL CAUSE** or telos. All operations of nature are for a final cause or end. This final cause, as mentioned above, is a concept of eudaimonia or personal and social flourishing. But one uglier implication of this teleological view, is that humans are by nature arranged according to classes. Slaves and barbarians occupy a fixed place, too, in a hierarchical view of human nature. MacIntyre argues that the pre-modern elitism has no place in postmodern understanding of the self.

MACINTYRE'S CRITIQUE OF MODERN CULTURE

Alasdair MacIntyre shares with Philippa Foot a distaste for the meta-ethical direction of the prevalent doctrine of **EMOTIVISM**-led philosophy in the mid-20th C. That direction ended in a blind alley of subjectivism and moral **RELATIVISM**.

A moral philosophy characteristically presupposes a sociology, argues MacIntyre, a point we shall return to shortly as it is the key insight he brings into how moral values are derived. But here MacIntyre accuses the emotivists (Ayer, Stevenson) of being blind to the social context of their own theory - blind to their own presuppositions. The social context of emotivism is based on the "obliteration of any genuine distinction between manipulative and non-manipulative social relations". To treat someone as an end is to give them good reasons for a moral action, but then to let them decide what action to take. To treat the same person as a means to some end (such as pleasure or profit) is to rob them of their dignity and expose them to manipulation.

What would the world look like through emotivist eyes? Emotivism turns us into consumers where the enemy to be assuaged is boredom. Hence there is a need for managers and bureaucrats to steer us by the utilitarian mechanisms of costs and benefits for external ends such as profit or growth. The manager, for example, "manipulates human beings into compliant modes of behaviour" (After Virtue, p27) and the focus is on external goods such as profit and performance and not the internal goods that define virtues for the business form of life.

In our own time the idea of "character" is coloured, argues MacIntyre, by emotivism. MacIntyre identifies three characters for special criticism - the bureaucrat, the rich playboy and the therapist. The bureaucrat manages sometimes irreconcilable desires, the playboy indulges them and the therapist picks up the casualties of our obsession with feeling. But morally speaking no-one has the intellectual tools to pass moral judgement and define behaviour as objectively wrong.

The self thus emotively conceived, is completely separated from social embodiments and lacks any rational history of its own. It is a rootless self, set loose on a tide of passion without any ethical rudder.

In pre-modern societies, in contrast, human beings inhabited roles which came from their context - I am brother, cousin and grandson, or member of a certain tribe. These are not characteristics that belonged to human beings accidentally, which need to be stripped away (by therapy) or indulged (by hedonism) in order to discover "the real me". In Aristotelian terms, they define our true natures and purpose - and without an understanding of the relation between a role and a value we lose sight of our true purpose and function.

THE REJECTION OF UTILITARIAN NATURALISM

Alasdair MacIntyre argued that the Enlightenment Project, with reason at its core, produced two failed attempts to justify values of right and wrong. One was the "moral fiction" of utilitarianism with its new teleology of pleasure and pain. The other was Kantian ethics, with its emphasis on a priori reason producing **UNIVERSALISABLE** maxims of practical reason. Both fail, MacIntyre argues, because they lack a coherent view of the self.

So instead of the Aristotelian idea of a human being fulfilling his or her essential nature, the rationalism of utilitarian and Kantian ethics presents the atomised self, either calculating according to desires (utilitarians) or reasoning by some abstract process (Kantian ethics). The individual is seen as a "moral atom" devoid of a social context or tradition.

Utilitarianism ultimately fails because the goal is indefinable. Happiness and pleasure as concepts beg the questions "whose happiness, and which form of pleasure?" Mill, himself, implies this when he defines pleasures in their higher (intellectual) and lower (bodily) forms. As MacIntyre points out, "the happiness of the way of life that belongs to the cloister is not the same as that which belongs peculiarly to the military life". (1997:64) There simply are no scales (hedons?) by which to measure the two and compare them. Thus happiness dissolves into a "pseudo-concept" - one which has resulted in beneficial social change, of course, but nonetheless change based on an empty idea, and the greatest happiness for the greatest number becomes an idea "without any clear content at all". So the utilitarians "purport to provide us with an objective and impersonal criterion, but they do not". (1997:70)

This leaves the individual in a position that is in the end incoherent. Emotivism has robbed us of meaningful language of moral discourse, because moral language simply expresses emotion and nothing else. And the legacy of utilitarian ethics is to leave us marooned on an island of supposed autonomous choice, seeking ways to avoid being manipulated by others. But at the same time:

> *We find no ways open to us except directing towards others those very manipulative modes of relationship which each of us aspires to resist. (1997:68)*

MACINTYRE'S POSTMODERN VIEW

The world of postmodernity is dominated by the idea of story or stories which emerge from different forms of life. Diversity is the natural feature of the postmodern world, and conflict between worldviews is an inevitable fact of moral life. Where tolerance may be seen to be a virtue, there nonetheless needs to be some objective basis, as Aristotle argued, for providing a **NATURALISTIC** account of what constitutes a virtue.

MacIntyre's account of the naturalistic origin of the virtues is brought out by his definition of virtue as:

> *An acquired human quality, the possession and exercise of which tends to enable us to achieve those goods which are internal to practices and the lack of which effectively prevent us from achieving any such goods. (1997:191)*

Where MacIntyre agrees with Aristotle that virtues are habits we acquire rather than are born with, he sees virtues arising out of **GOODS INTERNAL TO PRACTICES**. So for MacIntyre, "a moral philosophy ... characteristically presupposes a sociology". (1997:23)

The goods are radically contextual. The good of cricket, internal to the practice of cricket, may involve batting well, which itself depends on some idea of stroke play, timing, and judgement as well as fair play and observance of agreed rules. Match-fixing, ball-tampering, and sledging (the habit of abusing fellow players as they are about to make a stroke) are all clearly viewed as vices. The good of banking comes from the practice of trust, fairness, customer interest and prudence internal to banking, which so clearly were violated by the greed, mis-selling, and excessive risk-taking that caused the banking crisis of 2007-2008.

These internal or **INTRINSIC GOODS** are essentially different, argues MacIntyre, from the external goods of profit and shareholder returns in banking, or winning the league in cricket. The value of the virtues lies in their ability to dominate and control these external goods, rather than vice versa. Rather than reason dominating the passions, as in Aristotle's metaphysics, it is reason that causes the internal goods to overcome the negative possibilities of the external goods (in this banking case, the profit motive run wild, or in cricket, all the betting scandals which have emerged as distortions of the desire to win).

How does this differ from Aristotle? The source of the virtues in MacIntyre is the sociology of the group; in Aristotle, the biological **TELOS** of the human being and the rational activity of the soul, whereby the charioteer (reason) controls the unbridled passions and desires. To develop this, it is necessary to consider MacIntyre's second criticism, that Aristotle has an over-reliance on the idea of the static **POLIS** or city-state as the context of his ethics rather than a dynamic and ever-developing tradition of the social group.

POLIS VERSUS SOCIAL HISTORY AND TRADITION

Aristotle lived during the golden age of Athenian democracy. The city-state was a union of 300,000 people, around 6,000 of whom met on a hill to deliberate and vote on issues of common interest. The idea of social flourishing, so important to Aristotle, depends on the flourishing of this particular ideal of government by small unit, working co-operatively. As such it has little relevance to the complex world of competing interests which make up the postmodern state.

It is the nature of our lives embedded in a social context that brings out the key difference between Aristotle and MacIntyre. In the postmodern world with its diversity of practices, it is essential to explain how any one person can gain an idea of virtue. How do we order the internal scheme of the virtues, dependent as they are on different practices, into one coherent whole? How do we prevent our lives fragmenting into the banker, the cricketer, the family man, with different values and virtues applicable to each role? The end, remember, is a virtuous character, a whole, integrated, fulfilled, excellent human being.

It is here that MacIntyre employs the idea of "the unity of a narrative embodied in a single life" (AV p218). Here the question "what is good for me?" is closely linked, as in Aristotle, with the idea of what is good for humankind, and the idea of a lifetime quest. As we have seen Aristotle observe, emphasising the organic nature of the virtues:

> *Moreover, to be happy takes a complete lifetime; for one swallow does not make spring. (1926:1.7.1098a)*

But unlike Aristotle, with his fixed metaphysical biology, his common purpose and function for all human beings, the goal here is open-ended.

All of us are on a journey or quest to discover what is the best life for humankind. We inhabit two histories, says MacIntyre, a personal history of family and friends, and a moral **TRADITION** or moral history. The moral tradition arises out of the community I live in, as

> *I am born with a past; and to try and cut myself off from the past is to deform my present relationships. (1997:221)*

Part of this journey involves a criticism of my tradition as incomplete and partial, a tradition "with limitations" (1997:221). In MacIntyre's later work he reinterprets the idea of tradition to something much closer to

Aristotle. Instead of social practices he argues for traditions of intellectual enquiry (1988:349-369). He admits:

> *I now judge that I was in error in supposing an ethics independent of biology is possible. (Dependent Rational Animals: Why Human Beings Need The Virtues, 2001)*

The moral tradition of the Victorians, for instance, was very different from today's. Sex was seen as something dangerous, and more linked to the duty of reproduction than pleasure. Classes were rigidly separated by customs, dress and habits. Sunday was strictly observed as a day of rest. Modesty and thrift were prized. Emotions were suppressed. In recent years we have rightly become critical of many of the limitations of Victorian morality, but they remain part of our story, our self-understanding. They form part of our collective memory.

Is this account of evolving tradition very different from Aristotle's view of the city-state? Part of the difficulty is that Aristotle means two things by this phrase, at least as expressed in Politics - something close to what we mean by a state, but also, something comparable to what we mean by "community". This second usage (community) is much closer to MacIntyre's social practices than MacIntyre himself concedes. According to Nichomachean Ethics Book 10, it is the role of the polis to make people virtuous. It does this by reinforcing and making possible everything that contributes to the most excellent life: the family, friendship, regulation by agreed laws, and the teaching of right behaviour (1926:1104b 12-13), until the very activity itself becomes second nature and a source of pleasure. The polis is still the context of shared values, admittedly without the self-criticism and evolution MacIntyre describes as essential to a tradition.

In a famous passage Aristotle argues:

> *Argument and teaching are not effective in all cases; the soul of the listener must first be conditioned by habits to the right kind of likes and dislikes, just as the land must be cultivated before it is able to bring forth the seed. For a man whose life is guided by emotion will not listen to an argument that dissuades him, nor will he understand it. (1926:1179b, 23-281)*

Aristotle is arguing here that it is the polis that habituates us into right likes and dislikes, and from these spring right action. In other words, the polis, like the social practices, form the idea of good. MacIntyre concedes this point when he argues, "In Aristotle virtues find their place in the life of the city". (1997:150) Where MacIntyre departs from Aristotle is, however, in the idea of history that forms the tradition, the sense of an emerging and evolving sense of the common good which comes from sharing a story.

THE GOLDEN MEAN

Central to Aristotle's theory is the idea of the Golden Mean. Philosophers as distinguished as Bernard Williams have misunderstood this idea. Williams writes, "the mean is a depressing doctrine in favour of moderation. It is best forgotten". (Ethics and the Limits of Philosophy p36) This reduces the doctrine to a set of bourgeois practices along the lines of "Now dear, don't cry, because big boys don't cry." It is absolutely not what Aristotle argues.

Every virtue, says Aristotle, is a condition lying between two other states, one involving excess, and the other deficiency.

> *Excellence ... is a settled disposition determining choice, involving the observance of the mean relative to us, this being determined by reason, as the practically wise person would determine it. (1926:1106a26;1107a2)*

The idea of virtue sets us our target, says Aristotle, likening it to an arrow fired at a target. Then practical wisdom, **PHRONESIS**, fixes the exact form of the practice of the virtue, depending on the circumstances and what is appropriate. For example, if my child runs out in front of a car, it is appropriate to lose my temper and show extreme anger. If my child gets his maths homework wrong, it is not appropriate, as in Victorian times it seems it was, to hit them. Appropriate is the key word here.

So excellence, Aristotle says, aims at the **MEAN** which represents a judgement point chosen by the skilled thinker.

> *Excellence of character is concerned with emotions and acts, in which there can be excess or deficiency or a mean. For example, one can be frightened or bold, feel desire or anger or pity, and experience pleasure and pain generally, either more or less than is right, and in both cases wrongly. While to have these feelings at the right time, on the right occasion, toward the right people, for the right purpose and in the right manner, is to feel the best amount of them, which is the mean amount - and the best amount is of course the mark of excellence. Likewise, in acts there can be excess, deficiency and a mean ... Hence excellence is a mean state in the sense that it aims at the mean. (1926: 1106b,15-29)*

The Golden Mean therefore gives us the answer to the question - how do we apply the virtues? We apply them by cultivating the skill of phronesis to judge the mean. Yet MacIntyre gives the doctrine of the mean only a passing mention, which is strange, given its importance to Aristotle. He observes "Aristotle tries to use the notion of a mean between the more or the less to give a general characterisation of the virtues." (1997:154) The idea of the mean then forms no part of MacIntyre's own account. Why is this? And does MacIntyre replace the idea with something workable which you and I can use to make practical decisions?

Central to Aristotle's account, as we have seen, is his metaphysics. This has two parts, an argument about the general **ERGON**, or function, of human beings, which is to reason well, and a consideration of the makeup of the soul. Virtue, for Aristotle, is an activity of the soul in accordance with virtue. For MacIntyre it is a set of social practices which reinforce a practice and emerge from a tradition.

So Aristotle seems to argue that the soul is divided between the part that we share with the animals, the **NUTRITIVE** (growth) and **APPETITIVE** sides (food, sex, drink), and our desires, both of which need to be moralised or brought under the rule of reason. This practical reason tries to determine the right action, that is, one which accords with the overall goal of **EUDAIMONIA** as defined by the practice of the virtues. What, then, is the right type of anger to show, and the right degree of emotion to display? We cannot generalise about this or create an absolute rule to follow. We need to practise right judgement and so learn by reflection what is appropriate. And it will depend critically on our own individual strengths and weaknesses.

My argument here is that MacIntyre never develops any doctrine of the mean because he instinctively knows that it is so tailored to Aristotle's metaphysics that he would need to embrace some of the metaphysics to argue like this. But is Aristotle's account of the mean really at so much variance with insights from modern psychology? Consider how addictions of various kinds force people to extremes which destroy their ability to flourish - and addiction, remember, can be for things as diverse as alcohol, pornography and shopping. Extremes or deficiencies do rot the soul or if you don't like the word, let's use the Greek; they rot the **PSYCHE**: they rob us of something of our humanity and, in my opinion, they definitely prevent us becoming the most excellent people we could be.

BEGGING SOME QUESTIONS

The preceding analysis begs some questions which we can now briefly explore.

- Does MacIntyre's form of naturalism really work, given that we have so many competing ideas of what constitutes human flourishing? Recall that MacIntyre is scathing of the utilitarians for producing "moral fiction" of an idea of happiness. But isn't eudaimonia itself just another fiction? What gives eudaimonia specific content, especially when the therapists MacIntyre himself attacks present conflicting claims about the source of human flourishing? And if eudaimonia is not a fiction, what is to stop us making a concept so culturally-relative that we could justify almost anything as contributing to eudaimonia? (Aristotle justified slavery, for example, using his idea of proper function.)

- Is MacIntyre really a **RELATIVIST**, saying that the idea of goodness will always depend on a social context - a form of cultural relativism? If so, this again is a paradoxical position, because virtue ethics claims to have at its basis a revival of naturalism. Robert Wachbroit makes such a claim in an article in 1983 which MacIntyre tries to refute in an appendix to the second edition of After Virtue. If virtues are grounded in socially designed practices, then how do we resolve the issue when two such practices meet, both proclaiming a contradictory idea of the good? MacIntyre's reply is rather weak: he argues that if two such traditions conflict they will find "some common features". (1997:276)

- Is Aristotle's Golden Mean a better form of moral psychology than MacIntyre's group psychology, implied by the idea of "goods internal to practices", which could arguably justify practices of genocide in Nazi Germany? Using the cricketing analogy - isn't there some external criterion of goodness which we impose on Larwood's body liner form of bowling which argues it is intrinsically wrong because it causes pain? Isn't this true even if the cricketing authorities say body liners are "good" in the game of cricket? But MacIntyre rejects any kind of objective reason as part of the failed Enlightenment Project.

- Do we not, in fact, require some more objective metaphysics - an objective understanding of what makes up things that are good for the soul - but if we do, can we escape being snobs, who say in effect that the uneducated and unwise will never flourish, that they are doomed to a kind of ignorant determinism? Indeed, at least one author, Deborah Achtenberg of the University of Nevada, has argued that MacIntyre is actually putting forward another form of metaphysics in After Virtue.

Philippa Foot's Virtue Ethics

We did not sign up for the SS, and so they have condemned us to death. Both of us would rather die than stain our consciences with such horrific deeds.

So wrote a farm boy from the Sudetenland in a letter to his family shortly before his execution.

Philippa Foot discusses this letter in her final book Natural Goodness. The question it raises concerns the rationality of human choice. One of her central concerns is to discover the **NATURALISTIC** grounds for philosophy, where "naturalism" means "grounded in facts about the natural world and our true natures as human beings". Much like MacIntyre, she found her motive in a reaction to the subjectivist implications of **EMOTIVISM**.

She revealed in an interview with Julian Baggini just how the experience of Nazism appalled her and set her on a path to try to discover the source of objective value: "I was certain that it could not be right that the Nazis were convinced that there was no way that they were wrong."

She then notes a crucial distinction:

We cannot totally divorce the ideas of virtue and of happiness. There seems to be a necessary conceptual connection between them. And this is suggested by the fact that while one of the Letter Writers might have said, "I'm willing to sacrifice all my future happiness"; they might rather have said, "Happiness is

> *just not possible for me if I can only avoid death by going along with the Nazis, by betraying my comrades in the Resistance, or by obeying orders to join the SS". (The Philosophers' Magazine 21, 2003)*

The crucial distinction here is between happiness and self-interest. It is not logically impossible to argue that I prefer the path of virtue rather than personal happiness - or to put it another way, that the idea of happiness as an **INTRINSIC GOOD** must include something larger than just simply pleasure and self-interest. In this chapter I shall focus on Philippa Foot's last work, Natural Goodness, in order to explain how the virtues give us both a motive for acting morally (virtue is about the will), and reasonable steps to pursue the aims which we have first designated as "good" (a process of reasoning and giving reasons).

What will reason be based on? In arguing for naturalism, Foot is indeed arguing for an objective basis for morality - one based on natural facts - and it is with this concept that we begin our consideration of her views of the virtues.

VIRTUES AS OBJECTIVE STATES

The Sudetenland boy who preferred to die rather than serve the Nazis is indeed rational, but only insofar as we clarify the moral end which he seeks to pursue. This moral end is naturalistic, Foot argues, because (as with Aristotelian virtue ethics) it is grounded in some concept of human welfare. It is our shared understanding of welfare which gives morality such an objective basis as it has.

Foot argues that we make judgements of the goodness of living things by reference to a **TELEOLOGICAL** account of the life form of the species to which the thing belongs. For example, she takes the example of a peacock. The key question is: what function does its brightly coloured tail fulfil? Darwin used to observe that the very sight of a peacock's tail made him feel sick simply because he couldn't work out its function - until, that is, he came upon the idea of sex selection. The role of the tail is to attract pea-hens. The tail performs a key function in the sexual cycle of peacocks. Should a peacock fail to have a brightly coloured tail we would say it is a "bad peacock" and imply a value in this statement.

> *We start from the fact that it is the particular life form of a species of plant or animal that determines how an individual plant or animal should be. And all the truths about what this or that characteristic does, what its purpose or point is, and in suitable cases its function, must be related to this life cycle. The way an individual should be is determined by what is needed for development, self-maintenance, and reproduction. (2001:33)*

So if coloured tails are part of the objective facts about peacocks, and their goodness is derived from this function, what are these "objective facts" about the human condition which form the basis for moral norms?

Foot appeals to the Aristotelian idea of **EUDAIMONIA**, or flourishing, to explain this. A "good cactus" implies more than preferences we might have about cacti, but have within the idea of "good", "certain features of a good cactus that depend on what it is to flourish as a cactus" (2002: 141), which might include, for example, having healthy leaves of a certain colour. So there are "natural norms", which are unique to the human species, that ground morality in certain **NATURALISTIC** facts.

As in Aristotlean thought, human begins have certain functions that characterise them as "human". Given the diversity of human beings and cultures, can we identify criteria for "being human?" Foot (like Aristotle), argues for some form of teleological, ends-based reasoning.

VIRTUES AS CORRECTIVES

Virtues correct unruly passions - particularly when coupled with courage and temperance. Here Foot again follows Aristotle, but without his full metaphysical explanation of the soul. Courage corrects the vice of fear and temperance corrects the vices of lust or gluttony. It is only, Foot points out, because fear and the desire for pleasure tempt us that courage and temperance appear in our list of virtues. It is human nature that makes us fear and pursue pleasure and so virtue is necessary as a "corrective disposition". Here Foot agrees with Aquinas; he saw the passions as contrary to reason, and courage and temperance were needed to be steadfast in the face of danger or temptation. So, Foot concludes:

> *Virtues are corrective, each one standing at a point at which there is some temptation to be resisted or deficiency of motivation made good. (2002:325)*

But what of the "deficiency of motivation" or defect of the will? These defects apply especially to virtues of love and justice. Here it is not a temptation to do anything particular but a defect of not wanting to pursue these virtues in the first place. Echoing Joseph Butler's view of benevolence, Foot writes:

> *If people were as much attached to the good of others as they are to their own good there would be no more a general virtue of benevolence than there is a general virtue of self-love. (2002:327)*

Here we can see a problem with Foot's account of virtue which she herself acknowledges. If courage is seen as a corrective virtue for someone who is fearful, then the most virtuous person is the one who feels most fear but manages to overcome it. This contradicts an idea in Aristotle that accords with a common sense view of virtue - that the most admired virtuous person is someone like Nelson Mandela who seemed to be effortless in his virtues of patience, courage and understanding - to take pleasure in virtue that has become second nature.

VICE AS A DEFECT

If virtue is an objective state which aims at human flourishing, what does this make a vice? It is also a moral state with certain objective features, but here it is a defect not an asset. It is best defined negatively as something that we lack.

For example, the person who lacks wisdom will make a false judgement that things like wealth and social status are more important than family. This is more than weakness of will; the person who chooses a lifestyle devoted to pleasure has, according to Foot, a defect in his or her thinking process - it is a failure of reason.

> *While non-human animals go for the good that they see, human beings go for what they see as good. (2001:56)*

The difference between a moral vice and a natural defect (such as missing a limb) lies in our view about how we should act - in the deeds we choose and the decisions we make as a result of reason and emotion. As Hacker-Wright explains it:

> *Neo-Aristotelian ethical naturalism, as Foot pursues it, must be understood as a thesis concerning rationality, according to which practical rationality is species-relative ... nature is normative over our reasoning but not directly over our action. (2013:52).*

Foot follows Anscombe (Intention) in arguing that we have good reasons, for example, to be just and so to see justice as a virtue - it is in our interest. By analogy, being unjust is like injuring our own limbs deliberately. If we do what Aron Ralston did in the film 127 Hours and hack off our own limb because it is stuck in a crevasse, this is only because there is an overriding welfare reason for so doing which we can clearly explain. The higher aim is actually the same here as it is for naturalistic morality - that we want our bodies to function well.

Like John Rawls, Foot believes we rationally desire such **PRIMARY GOODS** as health, talents, education and this is something necessary because all rational people want this. Wanting these kind of goods is a universal feature of human life (note: echoes of natural law primary precepts there). Again John Hacker-Wright notes:

> *Foot's argument for the rational necessity of wanting limbs is tied to objective features of the human condition, specifically that limbs are normally essential to the execution of one's will and the fulfilment of our desires. (2013:53)*

By analogy with the limbs, we also desire virtues. Certain facts about human beings - such as our social nature - inform the virtues and give us good reasons for desiring them and classifying them as "good". Justice is one such example - it is a virtue impelled by its social context. A society without justice is a bad society and we can see this in features it possesses such as arbitrary imprisonment or a failure to observe property rights.

THE SUDETENLAND BOY AND PRACTICAL RATIONALITY

In Natural Goodness Foot argues that the Sudetenland boy who preferred death to serving the Nazi cause is displaying a rationality inherent in a true understanding of the virtues of justice and love. He is clearly not serving either his own desire for life or his own self-interest, but is willing to sacrifice these for a higher good..

However, he is showing a profoundly **TELEOLOGICAL** view of the nature of moral ends. These ends are good because they fulfil the conditions for human benefit, goodness and a flourishing life. Justice and love are two virtues which, if widely accepted, would greatly benefit the human race. They are, to use Foot's phrase, "naturally normative" - the value of goodness arises out of facts about the human condition and our true natures.

So, as we argued above, following Aristotle's view of virtue, what makes a virtue into something truly good is intrinsically linked to some idea of **EUDAIMONIA** or human flourishing. What practical rationality gives us, Foot argues, is a way of choosing right action which weighs moral considerations against self-interest or some other non-moral factor. The virtue of practical rationality (Greek **PHRONESIS**) allows us to weigh considerations such as family and desire to preserve our lives against justice and charity. She concludes, "It is not always rational to give help where it is needed, to keep a promise, or even always to tell the truth." (2001:11) We need to discern the appropriateness of our choice, and this is what makes our reasoning moral.

What makes the Sudetenland boy rational, then, is his personal assessment of what was the virtuous action, defined as one which most virtuous people would follow in similar circumstances. Here we could argue either of two things:

1. That the boy has a deeper view of happiness (what Foot calls "deep happiness") which includes some higher values, and that in being true to these values the martyred boy feels happy in some specific (obviously not pleasure-based) view of happiness.

2. That he discovered happiness "was not something possible for him" (2001:95) because of the external circumstances which were lacking (such as a just society where Jewish people were treated with dignity and respect). Foot takes this second view, and claims again an Aristotelian precedent, that some external conditions must be met for a human begin to attain happiness.

So goodness and objective happiness are essentially different, but related, ideas. Goodness is seen against an objective idea of the benefits of justice and love which the boy reasoned were higher goods than self-interest and hate. "Human beings go for what they see as good," Foot points out, which differentiates us from the animals "who only go for the good thing they see". (2001:56)

It is this ability to reason teleologically, on the basis of ends appropriate to our species, which makes practical rationality and Foot's description of it very close to Aristotle's explanation of the virtue of phronesis.

Christian Virtue Ethics

We have already seen how Aquinas takes the virtue ethics of Aristotle and develops it in a uniquely Christian way, whilst retaining the teleological worldview of the Greeks. This implies a continuity with the ideas of **PHRONESIS** (practical wisdom) and the proper function of human beings (to reason excellently); but then Aquinas applies principles from the divine law (the Bible) to generate what Aquinas calls **INFUSED VIRTUES** of love, faith and hope as described by Paul in 1 Corinthians 13. This gives Christian virtue ethics a particular twist; the virtues which we normally associate with Christian ethics, such as **AGAPE** love, obedience and humility would never have been accepted by Aristotle.

In this chapter we turn to Tom Wright's recent book on virtue, Virtue Reborn. In this, he takes and modifies some Aristotelian ideas such as **EUDAIMONIA**, the goal of personal and social flourishing, and explains how the Christian view of virtue radically alters the Greek worldview. In so doing he reminds us that Christian Virtue Ethics is a neglected strain within Christian thought, but one which very much arises out of the biblical account of morality.

THE REVOLUTION IN ETHICS

Tom Wright sees Christian virtue ethics as a twofold revolution. First of all, there is a revolution away from rules and commandments towards character formation, the practising of certain habits and disciplines and a new alphabet and grammar - his metaphor for a new way of talking and thinking about ethics. In this revolution it is as if we went to Russia and decided we needed to speak Russian; we would need not only the alphabet and grammar, and to practise hard, but also the "spirit of Russia". So it is with Christian Virtue Ethics; we need a new language, new practices but also the spirit of Christ himself.

The second revolution poses a challenge to the world: it is a revolution in the way Christians live within the world and relate to it. "The kingdom of God is among us," Jesus declares (Mark 1:12) and in so doing the rule of God breaks in in a new way, with "restorative justice and healing joy". (VR p62) But the focus is essentially different from Aristotelian virtue ethics. With Aristotle, the focus is the self (self-fulfilment as the goal of eudaimonia) whereas with the Christian, we tread the path of Jesus Christ who "emptied himself and took the form of a servant". (Philippians 2:7) Thus the "glory of virtue, in the Christian sense, is that self is not in the centre of the picture. God and God's kingdom are at the centre". (2010:62)

So when the Christian practices the habits of Christian virtue they reflect back God's glory to the world. And more than this, Christians build the very kingdom whose values they practice - a rule of God amongst us. Christians do this as a "royal priesthood" (1 Peter 2:9), a "holy nation", in the exalted state of people made in God's image to exercise "dominion" over the earth on God's behalf. This dominion or rule is characterised by loving stewardship and care rather than tyranny and oppression. So the Jesus revolution becomes the revolution of a kingdom breaking in now, in real time, reflecting the values and reality of heaven itself which will finally be revealed in its completeness when Christ returns in glory to remake the world in a great resurrection.

Jesus suffered, died and was raised in order to demonstrate the image of God in all its perfection. So he is never just an example to follow. He is a Lord to be worshipped and obeyed with the words: "The kingdom of God has come. Take up your cross and follow me!" (Matthew 16:24-6)

CHRISTIAN BLESSEDNESS

In Aristotelian ethics we have seen that the key goal or **TELOS** is eudaimonia, a state of personal and social flourishing which we gain by practising the virtues. This is described as **AGENT-CENTRED** because it stresses the formation of character of the moral agent and the fulfilment of self by a process of organic growth into the virtuous life.

The difference between Greek eudaimonia and Hebrew **BARUCH** (blessedness) is that blessedness comes from the action of a loving God who has expressed himself in the covenants. God's commitment to his people in the Hebrew Bible comes in a number of great epiphanies or revelations of his true nature. These epiphanies give us a clue to the very character of God himself so that:

> *Blessedness in the Hebrew sense of baruch ... includes "happiness" but as a result of something else - namely, the loving action of a Creator God ... fulfilling promises made to his ancient people contained in the covenant. (2010:90)*

And there is a second sense of this blessedness which reflects back on the social nature of the virtues. Christian blessedness becomes the fulfilment of the task which Israel was called to fulfil in the covenant as his chosen people, "worship, stewardship, generating justice and beauty: these are the primary vocations of God's redeemed people". (VR p72)

So the Christian Church, called to a life of following the Christ of the cross, become the new Israel, God's prototype community for the world renewed.

EUTHYPHRO'S DILEMMA

Although this is not discussed by Tom Wright, it is worth pausing for a moment to relate the idea of the church as the new Israel, called and commissioned to steward God's world and reflect his values, to Plato's **EUTHYPHRO**.

There is a dilemma here that can be expressed as something good because God has commanded it, or does God command it because it is good? The dilemma is this. If God commands something because it is good, then morality is independent of God and there is no such thing as a specifically Christian ethic. If something is good because God commands it then there are two problems. Firstly, many of the commands appear to be arbitrary without proper reasons (such as the command in Genesis that Abraham kill his son Isaac on the altar). Secondly, many of the commands appear empty of moral content, such as the command not to work on the Sabbath, or to wash yourself before entering the Temple.

However, Christian Virtue Ethics has a way out of Euthyphro's dilemma. As Tom Wright points out, the obsession with commandments and "thou shalt nots" is an essentially negative view of Christian morality and turns it into a rather miserable set of rules to obey.

In addition, the virtue ethicist might argue that the dilemma itself is misconceived because neither of the two options given about the nature of moral goodness is correct. It presents a fallacy, the fallacy of restricting the options similar to a fallacious choice such as "the earth is either flat or square". The world, and Christian ethics, is neither.

For the origin of Christian ethics, as presented in the great covenants of Deuteronomy or Exodus, is the character of God. God reveals himself as a God of virtue, particularly three great virtues, love, justice and faithfulness. In other words, the origin of Christian ethics comes from understanding the character of God as the definition and origin of goodness and then reflecting those characteristics back to the world. It is worth reading one of these great epiphanies in order to establish the power of this particular argument against Euthyphro.

> *4 So Moses chiselled out two stone tablets like the first ones and went up Mount Sinai early in the morning, as the Lord had commanded him; and he carried the two stone tablets in his hands. 5 Then the Lord came down in the cloud and stood there with him and proclaimed his name, the Lord. 6 And he passed in front of Moses, proclaiming, "The Lord, the Lord, the compassionate and gracious God, slow to anger, abounding in love and faithfulness, 7 maintaining love to thousands, and forgiving wickedness, rebellion and sin. Yet he does not leave the guilty unpunished; he punishes the children and their children for the sin of the parents to the third and fourth generation." (Exodus 34: 4-6)*

God comes down in a cloud and reveals himself to his chosen leader Moses. The first thing God does is reveal his name, **YAHWEH**, meaning "I am who I am". God the eternal, pre-existing creator then speaks and reveals his character. And God has the following virtues or characteristics.

LOVE - The Hebrew word is **HESED**, which means steadfast love, loyalty, loving-kindness. It appears 134 times in the Hebrew Bible. It is this covenant love which God abounds in. It means an absolute commitment to someone, without condition. It is this kind of love which means God cannot break his promises to Moses. The Christians, writing in Greek, take a Greek word for love and then infuse it with this sense of covenant commitment and unconditional loyalty. That word is **AGAPE**.

FAITHFULNESS - The Hebrew word is **EMETH.** This word implies integrity or consistency. It means God has to be true to himself but also true to his word. If God says something, he will faithfully fulfil it. If God says he will protect his people, then God will protect them always and absolutely. It has a Greek equivalent which the Christians use of Christ. That word is **ALETHEIA** (truth), and so Jesus is "full of grace and truth" (John 1:14) - the incarnation of the virtues of God himself.

JUSTICE - The Hebrew word **SEDEK** means righteousness, fairness or justice. But it also carries an additional meaning, that of giving an interest-free loan, for example, to those in need. In other words, it is not justice as retribution alone, but as fair distribution of benefits, too.

Notice an apparent paradox in this great epiphany. Although God forgives wickedness and sin and is "slow to anger", nonetheless God is angry (to paraphrase Aristotle) at the right time for the right reasons with the right people. He is angry with those who make the golden calf and worship it and orders them to be killed, and he is angry with the Amorites and other tribes of the coastal plains who worship false gods such as Baal. There is retribution in God's justice which people feared. Yet the reward for this loyalty and obedience on behalf of God's chosen people is that they will see awesome works and wonders performed.

> *8 Moses bowed to the ground at once and worshipped. 9 "Lord," he said, "if I have found favour in your eyes, then let the Lord go with us. Although this is a stiff-necked people, forgive our wickedness and our sin, and take us as your inheritance." 10 Then the Lord said: "I am making a covenant with you. Before all your people I will do wonders never before done in any nation in all the world. The people you live among will see how awesome is the work that I, the Lord, will do for you." (Exodus 34:8-10)*

THE MORAL DISCIPLINE OF A RENEWED MIND

Tom Wright argues that there is a Christian counterpart to the Greek telos of **EUDAIMONIA**, which is the concept of blessedness. Blessedness is the gift of the gracious God who has gone before us in Christ and who acts for us now through his Holy Spirit, bringing the kingdom of God, his rule, into being in our midst. The people of God are the reflection of kingdom virtues to the world. Christians embody them by God's grace and then they create them in good works reflecting love, faithfulness and justice, those three great kingdom values which reflect the character of God himself.

But just as there is a Christian idea that relates to eudaimonia, but liberates it from concentration on self, so there is a Christian idea of **PHRONESIS** or practical wisdom. For there is a strong theme in the New Testament that people need to "be renewed in the spirit of your minds". (Romans 12:1-2)

Because the age to come (the **ESCHATON**) has burst in through Jesus Christ, we are to think differently. As Tom Wright points out, our culture stresses feelings which override thoughts. The mind has become detached. But the Christian must think with sober detachment from the world. The phrase Paul uses in Romans 12 is "sober judgement", meaning moderate or temperate. There are echoes here of the **GOLDEN MEAN** arrived at in Aristotelian thought by the virtue of phronesis or practical wisdom.

Paul also asks us to "put on the new self which is being renewed in knowledge". (Colossians 3:4-5) The metaphor here is of clothing; we are to clothe ourselves in the virtues and renew the tired way we think by a new wisdom. But these virtues don't come naturally. It will require moral effort to "put to death" habits of the old nature and "put away" things that compromise our virtue. (Colossians 3:5; 3:8)

And finally, Tom Wright points out, if this challenge is not enough, Christians must fix their eyes on the way of the cross, the path of suffering. The ultimate expression of love will be a willingness to suffer and die if necessary for friends and also for strangers. The prototype and Lord is no less than the suffering servant of Isaiah 53, Jesus himself, whom Christians follow on a path to a hill of crucifixion called Calvary. Christians do so, displaying the virtues of patience, endurance and hope.

> *In order to develop Christian character the first step is suffering. (2010:153).*

THE PARABLE OF THE GOOD SAMARITAN AND CHRISTIAN LOVE

In order to ground the virtues now in the life and example of Jesus, I will take three parables to demonstrate how the parables of the kingdom reflect the virtues of the kingdom. But it is worth pausing before we discuss the first parable of the Good Samaritan, to consider a criticism Gilbert Harman makes of virtue ethics generally, the criticism that there is no such thing as stable characteristics in human beings and so the concept of character itself is flawed. He does this by discussing various famous experiments including the Seminary experiment of Darley and Batson (1973).

The researchers were seeking to test three hypotheses:

1. People thinking religious, "helping" thoughts would still be no more likely than others to offer assistance.

2. People in a hurry will be less likely to offer aid than others.

3. People who are religious in a Samaritan fashion will be more likely to help than those of a priestly or Levite fashion. In other words, people who are religious for what it will gain them, will be less likely to help than those who value religion for its own sake, or are searching for meaning in life.

The students were given questionnaires to fill in to show their religious disposition and determine who was most likely to be religious in a Samaritan fashion. This group was then told to go to another building and prepare a talk about seminary jobs, the other group a talk on the parable of the Good Samaritan, but on the way they encountered a man slumped in an alleyway. One control group was told they were late for the task and they should hurry up.

The key indicator of whether people helped was not whether the Good Samaritan was in their minds but whether they were in a hurry. Only 10% of those who were told to hurry up stopped to help, but 63% of those who were told there was no hurry stopped to render assistance. The conclusion seems to be that thinking about morality does not imply that people will act on moral beliefs. Or in a culture where we rush around, does ethics become an optional extra - a distraction from tasks we have set ourselves? It's worth reading the parable of the Good Samaritan again.

25 On one occasion an expert in the law stood up to test Jesus. "Teacher," he asked, "what must I do to inherit eternal life?" 26 "What is written in the Law?" he replied. "How do you read it?" 27 He answered, "Love the Lord your God with all your heart and with all your soul and with all your strength and with all your mind"[a]; and, "Love your neighbor as yourself." [Lev 19:18; Deut 6:5]28 "You have answered correctly," Jesus replied. "Do this and you will live." 29 But he wanted to justify himself, so he asked Jesus, "And who is my neighbour?" 30 In reply Jesus said: "A man was going down from Jerusalem to Jericho, when he was attacked by robbers. They stripped him of his clothes, beat him and went away, leaving him half dead. 31 A priest happened to be going down the same road, and when he saw the man, he passed by on the other side. 32 So too, a Levite, when he came to the place and saw him, passed by on the other side. 33 But a Samaritan, as he travelled, came where the man was; and when he saw him, he took pity on him. 34 He went to him and bandaged his wounds, pouring on oil and wine. Then he put the man on his own donkey, brought him to an inn and took care of him. 35 The next day he took out two denarii[c] and gave them to the innkeeper. 'Look after him,' he said, 'and when I return, I will reimburse you for any extra expense you may have.' 36 'Which of these three do you think was a neighbour to the man who fell into the hands of robbers?' 37 The expert in the law replied, 'The one who had mercy on him.' Jesus told him, 'Go and do likewise.'" (Luke 10, NIV)

Read through the lens of the seminary experiment, we can see that this parable is about the virtue of love and the true meaning of neighbourliness and whether we can act this way in a culture-obsessed time. This does not consist in what we profess to believe (the Priest and the Levite would have been well versed in the law) but in what we do. When Jesus is being "tested" the test is not just about whether he knows the law and the values of the kingdom. It is a test of interpretation, and Jesus' reply seems to suggest he was indeed a virtue ethicist; he is suggesting that the Good Samaritan had an integrity of character. He lived what he believed about agape love and did not allow distractions of busy-ness to affect his right judgement to act sacrificially; to bandage up the wounded man, put him on his donkey and then pay his hotel bill (which roughly translated would have come to around £250 today).

Go, says Jesus, and put these kinds of kingdom values into practice with the sort of flexibility and right judgement that shows you understand them.

THE PARABLE OF THE SOWER AND CHRISTIAN FAITH

To what extent does Jesus' teaching inform us of the meaning of faith (the second virtue mentioned by Paul in 1 Corinthians 13)? Faith is closely linked to the characteristic of God revealed to Moses, that of faithfulness (Hebrew, **EMETH**). Faith means sticking by some principle of rightness even when it is not in the believer's interest to do so. It means holding on to truth when truth seems to be mysterious or even inconsistent. It means relying on the source of values and virtues, and trusting God himself, and the power of the Holy Spirit to bring to fruition the values of the kingdom in the Christian's life. This is best illustrated by the parable of the Sower. (Mark 4: 4-20)

4 Again Jesus began to teach by the lake. The crowd that gathered around him was so large that he got into a boat and sat in it out on the lake, while all the people were along the shore at the water's edge. 2 He taught them many things by parables, and in his teaching said: 3 "Listen! A farmer went out to sow his seed. 4 As he was scattering the seed, some fell along the path, and the birds came and ate it up. 5 Some fell on rocky places, where it did not have much soil. It sprang up quickly, because the soil was shallow. 6 But when the sun came up, the plants were scorched, and they withered because they had no root. 7 Other seed fell among thorns, which grew up and choked the plants, so that they did not bear grain. 8 Still other seed fell on good soil. It came up, grew and produced a crop, some multiplying thirty, some sixty, some a hundred times." 9 Then Jesus said, "Whoever has ears to hear, let them hear." (Mark 4, NIV)

Who are the fruitful ones? Jesus explains that they are those who hear the word, accept it, and bear fruit as a result. The acceptance here implies they believe (have faith) and obey (put it into action). And what is the fruit? Some have interpreted this fruit as the sevenfold fruit of the Holy Spirit which Paul mentions in Galatians 5:22 - the virtues which the Holy Spirit brings to fruition in those who are faithful - love, joy, peace, forbearance, kindness, goodness, faithfulness, gentleness and self-control. Notice that at least three of these are Aristotelian virtues (forbearance, goodness and self-control which are usually translated as fortitude, goodness and temperance in Nichomachean Ethics). What seems clear is that the fruit is produced by God, "infused" as Aquinas puts it, in those who believe and then act.

THE PARABLE OF THE PRODIGAL SON AND CHRISTIAN HOPE

Finally, how does the third virtue Paul mentions in 1 Corinthians 13, that of Christian hope, reflect itself in the teaching of Jesus? The answer is given in the parable of the Prodigal Son (Luke 15:11-32).

> "*11 Jesus continued: 'There was a man who had two sons. 12 The younger one said to his father, "Father, give me my share of the estate." So he divided his property between them. 13 Not long after that, the younger son got together all he had, set off for a distant country and there squandered his wealth in wild living. 14 After he had spent everything, there was a severe famine in that whole country, and he began to be in need. 15 So he went and hired himself out to a citizen of that country, who sent him to his fields to feed pigs. 16 He longed to fill his stomach with the pods that the pigs were eating, but no one gave him anything'.*
>
> *17 'When he came to his senses, he said, "How many of my father's hired servants have food to spare, and here I am starving to death! 18 I will set out and go back to my father and say to him: 'Father, I have sinned against heaven and against you. 19 I am no longer worthy to be called your son; make me like one of your hired servants'." 20 So he got up and went to his father'.*
>
> *'But while he was still a long way off, his father saw him and was filled with compassion for him; he ran to his son, threw his arms around him and kissed him'.*

21 'The son said to him, "Father, I have sinned against heaven and against you. I am no longer worthy to be called your son." 22 But the father said to his servants, "Quick! Bring the best robe and put it on him. Put a ring on his finger and sandals on his feet. 23 Bring the fattened calf and kill it. Let's have a feast and celebrate. 24 For this son of mine was dead and is alive again; he was lost and is found." So they began to celebrate. 25 Meanwhile, the older son was in the field. When he came near the house, he heard music and dancing. 26 So he called one of the servants and asked him what was going on. 27 "Your brother has come," he replied, "and your father has killed the fattened calf because he has him back safe and sound." 28 The older brother became angry and refused to go in. So his father went out and pleaded with him. 29 But he answered his father, "Look! All these years I've been slaving for you and never disobeyed your orders. Yet you never gave me even a young goat so I could celebrate with my friends. 30 But when this son of yours who has squandered your property with prostitutes comes home, you kill the fattened calf for him!"

31 "My son," the father said, "you are always with me, and everything I have is yours. 32 But we had to celebrate and be glad, because this brother of yours was dead and is alive again; he was lost and is found".'" (Luke 15, NIV)

The parable intends to link God to the Father and the reckless son to human beings. Christian hope is reflected in both the attitude of the Father and of the son.

To the Father, the son has disappeared with all his inheritance into a far country. The Father doesn't know if he is dead or alive. But he continues to believe and hope, to watch and wait and spots him even when he is a long way off. The Father never stops believing that the son will one day return and everything will be well again. This is Christian hope in the **ESCHATON** - despite all the evidence to the contrary of human beings' reckless sin, one day the world will be restored and a new community re-established - one of music and dancing and celebration.

Then there is the hope of the son. He knows he has sinned and has become the lowest moral being, feeding unclean pigs with apparently no hope of redemption. But there is hope. He says "I will go and confess to my father and tell him I am no longer worthy to be called his son." In other words, the son repents, which means "to turn around". So on an individual level there is always hope, even for the worst sinner (or the worst addict), that we can be restored. No matter how awful the circumstances, the son hopes for restoration because he believes in the essential goodness of the Father's character.

So what is this hope? This virtue is no other than holding on to the trust that God will one day fulfil the promises inherent in his character of goodness, love, faithfulness and justice.

God will restore what Paul calls the groaning creation, which is painfully bringing to birth the reign of God. And Christians too groan, like the Prodigal Son as they await adoption as sons and daughters of God and believe in the eschaton, the renewed creation which Christ will bring at his second coming. So, argues Paul, and Aquinas, and anyone who meditates on Christian virtue:

> *These three things abide: faith, hope and love. But the greatest of these, is love. (1 Corinthians 13:13)*

CONCLUSIONS

In Virtue Reborn, Tom Wright is arguing for a reworking of Christian ethics along the lines of a rediscovery of Christian virtue. These virtues are kingdom values which stem from the character of God himself. They are, he argues, deeply counter-cultural values because culture, invaded by beliefs about individualism, sees my salvation, my healing, my faith as central, and heaven as some gift for those who believe.

On the contrary, argues Tom Wright, Christian Virtue Ethics sees the community of Christ, the body incarnate in the world, as the demonstrator of kingdom values here and now. So Christians restore the broken, feed the hungry, become peacemakers by working at and practising the virtues of hope, faith, love and justice in action now. Christians try to put into practice the beatitudes of the Sermon on the Mount and so create blessedness (the Christian word for **EUDAIMONIA**) now. These small actions anticipate the great restoration of the second coming of Christ, when in resurrection glory he will judge and remake creation.

The virtues of Christian ethics are demonstrated both in the character of God (as in the epiphanies or revelations of his character, such as Exodus 34, when the covenant is made with Moses) and in the character of the Son of God who is revealed to us as "full of grace and truth" - a gift of God's generous grace in order to show how much "God so loved the world" (John 1; John 4).

Christians cannot hope to be exactly like Jesus (that would mean a perfection impossible for human beings), but they can be inspired by his example and his values and with the help of the Holy Spirit build the kingdom of God which first broke through in Jesus' first coming.

In this way Christians can practise an "eschatologically driven virtue ethic" (2010:149) - that is to say, one driven by hope that God, like the waiting father of the Prodigal Son parable, will again act in history to restore a broken world just as he first acted in Christ's life, death and resurrection.

Applied Virtue Ethics

In this chapter we will consider three applied ethical issues, those surrounding abortion, pre-marital sex and the environment, in order to answer the question "Is virtue ethics of any practical use?"

It is helpful to focus on specific arguments and so I have selected two articles by Rosalind Hursthouse (1991, 2006 reprinted in a book selection), a virtue ethicist, and one book by John Grabowski (2003). In examining their arguments we may discover some principles by which to apply virtue ethics to practical cases.

ABORTION AND THE VICE OF CALLOUSNESS

When we consider ethical issues surrounding abortion, we often start by considering the moral status of the foetus and whether the foetus should be given rights as a human person, or at least a potential human person. Hursthouse rejects such speculations as metaphysical and therefore a matter of beliefs, rather than philosophy, so "fundamentally irrelevant".

> *The morality of abortion is commonly discussed in relation to just two considerations: first, the status of the foetus ; secondly, women's rights ... virtue theory quite transforms the discussion of abortion by dismissing the two familiar dominating considerations as, in a way, fundamentally irrelevant. (1991:233-4)*

The issue of women's rights is irrelevant because someone may do something vicious even when exercising a right. For example, I may have the right to choose an abortion in law, but to do so just because I wish to take a holiday in Lanzarote next month would appear to lack virtue. The reasons appear to be entirely selfish and callous so that:

> *In exercising a moral right I can do something cruel, or callous, or selfish, light-minded, self-righteous, stupid, inconsiderate, disloyal, dishonest - that is, act viciously. (1991:235)*

Therefore the status of the foetus is fundamentally irresolvable. What concerns the virtue ethicist is what habits of action produce a flourishing life (**EUDAIMONIA**). So the primary question for Hursthouse in any issue is the question: "In having an abortion in these circumstances, would the agent be acting virtuously or viciously or neither?" (1991:236)

She argues that it's possible that a woman having an abortion could be acting virtuously or viciously and "there is no single right answer, but a variety of particular answers". What we need to do is disentangle the reason behind the action, to examine motives and wider facts and circumstances surrounding each case, "the facts that most human societies are and have been familiar with". (1991:236) Many reasons, she argues, may not be good moral reasons at all; for example, a desire for freedom she describes as selfishness; reasons such as "family circumstances" or "inability to cope with disability" (to cite two criteria for abortion in the 1967 Abortion Act) she sees as forms of cowardice.

Even when circumstances make abortion the right thing to do, she argues that this is often a sign of a severely flawed environment.

> *For, by virtue of the fact that a human life has been cut short, some evil has probably been brought about, and that*

> *circumstances make the decision to bring about some evil the right decision will be a ground for guilt if getting into those circumstances in the first place itself manifested a flaw in character. (1991)*

In other words, even if the abortion is the virtuous thing to do, it may only be so because of unvirtuous behaviour on your part (having casual sex, hanging out in a bad place, failure to use contraception, etc).

Moreover, in examining the facts surrounding a desire to abort we need to consider not just the biological facts about a mother's health, but the emotional facts surrounding each case. How do thoughts and feelings affect the decision? Hursthouse stresses that the virtuous person considers all the evidence before making a decision and decides how to apply values thought of as virtuous to this particular case. The morality of abortion therefore rests in having the right attitude to the facts surrounding each case:

> *How do these [familiar biological] facts figure in the practical reasoning, actions and passions, thoughts and reactions, of the virtuous and the non-virtuous? What is the mark to having the right attitude to these facts and what manifests having the wrong attitude to them? (1991:237)*

Because it involves the killing of a potential human being, and in that sense "taking a life", abortion is a serious matter. To be light-hearted, cruel, unfeeling is to take a vicious attitude to it. She concludes, no doubt having the utilitarians in her sights with their **INSTRUMENTAL** view of happiness:

> *To think of abortion as nothing but the killing of something that does not matter, or as nothing but the exercise of some right ... or as the incidental means to some desirable state of affairs, is to do something callous and light-minded, the sort of thing that no virtuous and wise person would do. (1991:237-238)*

Hursthouse continues by giving examples of real moral goods which may be included in our decision: a mother of several children who "fears that to have another will seriously affect her capacity to be a good mother to the ones she has" (1991:241); "a woman who has been a good mother and is approaching the age at which she may be looking forward to being a good grandmother" (1991:241); "a woman who discovers that her pregnancy may well kill her" and "a woman who has decided to lead a life centred around some other worthwhile activity or activities with which motherhood would compete". (1991:242)

Decisions which she sees as morally bad include those with "worthless" goals such as "'having a good time' or for the pursuit of some false vision of the ideals of freedom or self-realisation". (1991:242) She criticises those who have a romantic dream "of having two perfect children, a girl and a boy, within a perfect marriage, in financially secure circumstances, with an interesting job of one's own". (1991:242) These are morally wrong because they go against the objective facts of child-rearing and motherhood.

Does Hursthouse's view of abortion add up to a coherent virtue ethical response to a complex question? Jo Kornegay argues that Hursthouse slips a view of the moral status of the foetus in by the back door. We can test this by asking the question: would the killing of a live infant be justified in circumstances such as pursuing a career as a top consultant (or any other "worthwhile activity")? Kornegay concludes:

> *Clearly, for Hursthouse, the status of the foetus is lower than that of a typical adult or an infant. Her examples of reasons needed to justify an abortion would not be adequate to justify homicide or infanticide ... she must attribute a sufficiently low status to the foetus to avoid the implication that abortion is an unjust killing. (2011:55)*

Indeed, Kornegay goes on to argue, Rosalind Hursthouse appears to hold a developmental view of the foetus whereby a foetus under 7 weeks old is of less moral value than a foetus that is nearer full term. Kornegay herself believes that Hursthouse's view can be saved by reference to certain natural facts about the foetus which apply at around 24 weeks which give the foetus greater moral status. These include:

> *The various capacities for conscious experience; social responsiveness; appetites; emotions (including pain and preferential, behavioural responses); memory; learning, as well as the foundations for focusing on, and understanding, language. (2011:14)*

However, as Mathew Lu points out in a research paper:

> *Traditionally, the language of "potentiality" and "actuality" was tied to an Aristotelian metaphysics, and in this particular case we would analyse foetal status in terms of natural kinds. The foetus is (actually) a human being from the moment of its ontogenesis (at conception) because it is (actually) a member of that natural kind. It is true that it is an immature member of that kind, and cannot exercise some capacities commonly associated with (or even essential to) that kind, such as rationality.*

> *However, the same can be said of an infant (or young child). In this particular individual the essential capacities of its kind are in potentiality; the salient point is that this is so only in virtue of the fact that it (already) is a member of this kind.*

In other words, once we appear to accept the developmental view of the foetus, as Hursthouse implicitly does, we are accepting a view of natural kinds and their functions which seems to commit us to the very metaphysical position (as with Aristotelian virtue ethics) that Hursthouse rejects.

PRE-MARITAL SEX AND THE VIRTUE OF CHASTITY

The virtue of chastity involves the moderation by good habits of sexual appetites, controlled by right reason or the intellectual virtue of **PHRONESIS**. Chastity is therefore closely allied to temperance - a moderation of unbridled appetites, and according to John Krabowski it is "one of the most misunderstood and maligned virtues in contemporary culture". (2003)

Why should we be "chaste"? Isn't this an outdated Christian idea? Arguably not. In a culture awash with sexualised images and unrestricted access to a variety of media, the need for self-control of sexual passion for some higher end of human flourishing couldn't be more relevant. Paul expresses the universal need for sexual self-control in this way: "Flee from sexual immorality! Every other sexual sin is outside the body, but he who sins sexually sins against his own body." (1 Corinthians 6:18) What could Paul possibly mean by "sinning against your own body"?

There are psychological effects of, for example, viewing pornography or engaging in promiscuous pre-marital sex. These practices affect our feelings about ourselves (they may lower our self-image or turn the sexual partner into an object of pleasure, so dehumanising them), and equally seriously, they may make it harder to form permanent, trusting, faithful relationships. Are these sorts of relationships necessary for human flourishing? Again, arguably so, for you don't have to be a believer to agree with Genesis - "it is not good for humankind to be alone" (Genesis 2:18). We all need partners we can rely on for mutual support and upbuilding. The path of the sexually intemperate person is a lonely path.

The role of the virtue of chastity is, therefore, to get our feelings under control of our reason so we can make real choices about our sexual partners and not be enslaved and dehumanised by lust. The addict is bereft of human dignity, the dignity of choice (be they alcohol, sex or gambling addicts). As John Grabowski explains:

> *Chastity as integral to healthy psychosexual development is opposed to both repression (denial of sex) and sexism (denigrating and seeking power over members of the opposite sex). (2003:90)*

One of the difficulties we have in understanding the meaning of chastity as self-control rather than abstinence is the negative effect of Augustine's teaching on **CONCUPISCENCE** - his word for sexual desire, passion and longing. Augustine saw lust entering the world after the Fall in Genesis 3, when the man and woman saw each other's nakedness "and were ashamed". So Adam and Eve became incapable of refusing their bodies' demands and hated themselves for it, so they made aprons of leaves to hide their shame. Human genitals became out of control "as clear testimony of the punishment of man's first sin".

Therefore the whole of humankind becomes a **MASSA DAMNATA**, a "crowd condemned". Lust, argues Augustine, infects all other desires, distracts us from the path of reason and becomes a prime mover of the human will. Others took their war on lust more seriously: St Benedict tore his clothes off and rolled in a thorn bush until he forced the lust out through his wounds; Saint Alexandra walled herself up for ten years in a tomb and Origen castrated himself. For Augustine, even sex within marriage for procreation has warnings attached:

> *In marriage, sexual intercourse for the purpose of conceiving children has no fault attached to it. But used to satisfy lust, even with a spouse, it is venial sin. (On the Good of Marriage)*

It is refreshing then, when we read Aquinas, to find a more positive view of sexual desire. Chastity perfects our sexual appetites and brings them under the control of reason, so that they are moderated to the higher end of blessedness, argues Aquinas. There is nothing wrong with sexual pleasure; it is the nature of the act which defines whether it is wrong. Wrong actions are those which do not relate to the true purpose of sex, which is to beget children within a lifelong union of faithful love.

This ordering of sex towards its true end does have certain paradoxical outcomes, namely that Aquinas sees masturbation as more sinful than rape. The forms of lust that violate the natural procreative purpose include homosexual sex or sex with contraception. We find echoes of this view in the controversial encyclical Humanae Vitae, which describes homosexual sex as "intrinsically disordered" (1967). Sex before marriage, however, does not break this natural function and so is seen as less morally serious.

Pope John Paul II builds on Aquinas' insights in arguing that chastity is integrated with love (Love and Responsibility, 1991). Chastity brings self-control to our imaginations in order to "affirm the value of the person in every situation". We can be chaste, argues John Paul, whenever sexual union is characterised by self-giving and respect for the other person. Chastity is as much about sexual feelings within marriage, which are directed and controlled appropriately, as it is about relations between unmarried people. In contrast, our culture turns sex into a commodity to be consumed and the enflaming of lust as a marketing strategy.

> *This consumer orientation of sensuality is a matter of spontaneous reflexes, and is not primarily an evil thing but a natural thing ... Sensuality expresses itself mainly in an appetitive form: a person of the other sex is seen as an "object of desire" specifically because of the sexual value inherent in the body itself, for it is in the body that the senses discover that which determines sexual difference, sexual "otherness". (1960: 106-107).*

The human person, however, should be viewed as whole, and, as with virtue ethics, desires and pleasures should be integrated towards the ultimate end of God-ordained happiness. So the body:

> *Cannot be an object for use. Now, the body is an integral part of the person, and so must not be treated as though it were detached from the whole person: both the value of the body and the sexual value which finds expression in the body depend upon the value of the person ... a sensual reaction in which the body and sex are a possible object for use threatens to devalue the person. (1960:107)*

So a passionate sexual relationship that has self-giving at its heart is perfectly moral. Does this mean that John Paul approves of extra-marital sex when performed in the context of a loving, committed relationship? John Paul argues not (although I think the non-Christian could argue this) because the God-ordained nature of marriage is as a covenant reflecting lifelong unconditional commitment of one person to the other. The great covenant value is fidelity or faithfulness, expressed in the passages of the Hebrew Bible where God is revealed as "abounding in steadfast love and faithfulness" (Exodus 34:6). These covenants or commitments made between God and humankind have virtues at their very core.

John Grabowski agrees. His morality of sex echoes the views of Tom Wright's Virtue Reborn. For it is against the supreme virtue of covenant commitment and love that sexual relations should be understood. Covenant is the supreme virtue that chastity strengthens. Covenants are "cut" in the Hebrew Bible - sometimes literally as in Genesis15:18 where Abraham has to cut three animals in half and walk between them to symbolise the unbreakable nature of this new relationship with God.

The argument against pre-marital sex is this: it cannot, by its very nature, reflect true covenant because it is not "cut" or sealed by public vows of lifelong faithfulness - even if this may be the intention of a committed couple. And casual pre-marital sex is a venial sin (meaning a pardonable sin which doesn't eternally cut us off from God) because it is driven by a lust which goes against right reason.

Only such vows made before God and the general public as a public covenant truly reflect the exalted God-given state of marriage as the context of sexual relations, where a "wife leaves her family and cleaves to her husband and the two become one flesh" (Genesis 2:24 is echoed by Jesus in Matthew 19:5). This reflects the covenant between God and humankind whereby Christians leave the false gods and cleave to a union with the one true God, the source of love and faithfulness. So the idea of a marriage covenant gives marriage its **SACRAMENTAL** nature - meaning that marriage becomes a source of God's grace and a way that He blesses human beings and leads them on a path to a fulfilled and happy life.

ENVIRONMENTAL VIRTUE

Virtues express themselves in what virtuous people do, and vices in what virtuous people avoid doing. This may sound like tautology, but not when it is linked to the ultimate goal or **TELOS** of the flourishing individual, the flourishing society and the flourishing world.

We would therefore expect virtues to reflect themselves in virtuous activity, but the nature of that activity to be contextual. In other words it depends on the context (what MacIntyre calls a "form of life") what virtue we apply and what practical action we take. This is the decision of **PHRONESIS** or practical wisdom. Not only does this determine which virtue we identify as important, but it enables us to determine new virtues when faced with new issues. This, argues Rosalind Hursthouse, is exactly what is required when we face the issues produced by climate change, or the use of agrochemicals on crops, to take two examples.

The use of agrochemicals can be taken to illustrate how virtues and practical action go together. If in Argentina it can be established that the spraying of agrochemicals on soya crops is producing cancers in children and miscarriages in pregnant women, then the virtuous person would act to prevent these things happening under the virtue of care and compassion. But go one stage back and we discover chemical companies protesting that "we take the welfare of our communities very seriously". They are arguing for the virtue of care. However, what are they doing to prove that they care in the practice of this virtue?

We suspect (perhaps cynically) that in business, interests such as the desire for profit come in the way of the virtues. So we would ask whether these same companies are spending money to research the high incidence of cancers among children. After all, if there is a link, it must be proved. But if these same companies are spending no money on such research even in the presence of a statistical anomaly of high cancer rates, we would accuse them, quite rightly, of having the vice of indifference. We would say, objectively speaking, that they do not care.

The question therefore arises: Why should we care about the environment, and how; if we can establish that carelessness will produce the destruction of the planet and hence the end of the human race (an extreme form of lack of flourishing), then what virtues do we need to make sure such defects are addressed?

It is here that Rosalind Hursthouse (2006) acknowledges an indebtedness to the environmentalist Paul Taylor. Taylor introduces an idea which we could ascribe as a virtue, the value of "respect for nature".

> *One sees one's membership in the Earth's Community of Life as providing a common bond with all the different species of animals and plants that have evolved over the ages. One becomes aware that, like all other living things on our planet, one's very existence depends on the fundamental soundness and integrity of the biological system of nature. When one looks at this domain of life in its totality, one sees it to be a complex and unified web of interdependent parts. (Taylor, 1986:44)*

Paul Taylor is arguing for an "ultimate moral attitude" to nature, based on the interdependency of all parts within the whole, including human life, which causes us to talk in terms of a "whole earth community". So the integrity of the biological system has an element of intrinsic goodness. This goodness is, as Hursthouse points out, based on an Aristotelian idea that "any living thing has a **TELOS** - a good of its own - as such, any living thing can be benefited or harmed". (2006:163)

Hursthouse takes up this point about the link between virtue and the place of the earth community to argue for two new virtues: respect for nature and a "sense of wonder". Taylor, interestingly, draws his inspiration from Kant, who sees respect for persons as persons as the foundation for his second formulation of the **CATEGORICAL IMPERATIVE**, ie "do not treat people simply as a means to an end but always also as an end in themselves". Can this not be extended to a more universal, less anthropocentric (human-centred) formula, which of course, is exactly what Kant fails to do, to respect nature as nature? That is certainly one argument for establishing an environmental ethic.

Hursthouse argues, however, that only virtue ethics can identify and inculcate these right attitudes to nature. Only virtue ethics can supply the motivation to be moral that Kantian ethics lacks. This is because a virtue is set within the whole of life and is a lifetime quest of creating good habits. The habits are linked to the richer goal or telos of a thriving, flourishing planet. In this way virtues motivate us and guide our conduct towards the environment. But this involves a revolution in our naturally anthropocentric values.

> *Coming to see oneself as sharing a "common bond" with all living things would involve a radical change in our perceptions and emotions, of one's reasons for action and one's action. (2006:163)*

In other words, Hursthouse argues that virtue ethics can supply the motivation that Kantian ethics or utilitarianism lack. For virtue ethics goes one stage back, as it were, in arguing for virtues inculcated from childhood in the training and development of character. She argues that this can be done if we reorientate education around some core skills which help children identify what actions "harm" or "kill" or "cause pain" or "feed", as linked to the proper purpose of the living thing in question and identification of certain **NATURALISTIC** features of our behaviour.

A practical example might help to ground this idea. Suppose I see a child pulling a cat's tail. The first step is to establish that this causes pain (a naturalistic feature of the action of tail pulling). The next step is to link the action to the vice of cruelty. So we might argue "Don't pull Tabby's tail, it's cruel!" We have given a reason to justify a rule which would be followed by the virtuous person: "Don't pull tails."

How could this be applied as an idea to the larger issues of climate change and pollution? Many people assent to the idea that "pollution is wrong". But does this guide actions in a practical way? Take for example, the Glastonbury festival (my example, not Hursthouse's), brimming with environmental idealists. How many tons of litter are picked up at the end of the festival? How many caravans, tents, bicycles are simply abandoned and therefore wasted? This would seem to give force to Hursthouse's argument that we need to teach new virtues and vices in such a way that they become second nature (not to waste, not to pollute with litter).

A second virtue alongside the respect for nature, she argues, would be a sense of wonder. This is linked to a proper appreciation of beauty within the environment. My respect for a tree stems from an appreciation not just of the place of the tree in the ecosystem (see above), but the inherent goodness of a tree's beauty. This beauty is not just to do with appearance, though it includes that, but in the beauty of its function - its ability to recycle carbon dioxide as the earth's lungs, and to generate oxygen which sustains all life. Such reverence for nature, an ability to feel awe, could again be inculcated by education at an early age - if only we could move education away from its instrumental, means-to-an-end obsession with attaining some target of exam success.

In other words, if all of us meditated hard on our contribution to educating and practising the virtue of wonder, we could develop the practical wisdom to "feel wonder in the right way, towards the right objects, for the right reasons, to the right degree, and to act accordingly". (2006:161) And would we thereby change our practices? Would such character formation change behaviour at pop festivals or in the way we choose a new car or the way we drive it? Of course the answer is "yes", for that is the strength of the idea of virtue - it gives reasons and it forms motives which help alter character and guide practical action.

Evaluating Virtue Ethics

JAMES RACHELS AND THE INCOMPLETENESS CRITICISM

James Rachels (1993:177-179) argues that virtue theory, although having many advantages over **DEONTOLOGY** (such as supplying strong motives for action), is incomplete as it stands because it cannot answer two fundamental problems in moral decision-making: the question of what to do when two virtues conflict, and an explanation of the place of rules - deontology - in moral decision-making. Let's consider each in turn.

Moral conflicts arise when two equally good values come into direct collision and we are forced to choose between them. For example, my friend asks me to cover for him when flying to Germany to watch his favourite football team, Bayern Munich. The head teacher asks me "Where is John?" and I reply "He's sick with a migraine." I make this decision to lie in this case where the virtue of honesty conflicts with the virtue of loyalty to my friend.

We might observe at the outset that this problem seems to afflict all moral theories which produce some clear norm of goodness. Kant, for example, in a notorious essay, claimed we should always tell the truth to an axe-murderer at our door who asks us if our friend is hiding in the house. We are supposed to answer "yes", even though this offends against both our common sense and his own theory that you should **UNIVERSALISE** your action and so accept that it's fine for me to be killed if I was in the position of the friend cowering behind the sofa.

That, however, doesn't let virtue ethics off this particular hook. What then are the details of James Rachels's argument? The reason why someone should not lie is that to do so would be dishonest. Rachels therefore asks:

> *Isn't an honest person simply someone who follows such rules as "do not lie"? It is hard to see what honesty consists in if it is not the disposition to follow such rules. (1993:177).*

I think Rachels mis-states the process of reasoning within virtue ethics here. For the virtue ethicist is never arguing that the same person in the same situation will behave in the same way - for example, holding absolutely to the "no lying" rule. If the no lying rule is just a "rule of thumb", or guideline, then it isn't really a rule at all in a meaningful way. Indeed, the argument of virtue ethics is that only the wise person, skilled in **PHRONESIS**, will know what to do when two virtues apparently conflict. In other words, if there is a rule at all in virtue ethics it is the more general rule: "always do what a wise person would do".

Does this get us out of the second problem of conflicting virtues and moral dilemmas? Again, I think it does if we keep the end of **EUDAIMONIA** in view. This is because virtue ethics does have this one intrinsic value at its heart. The objective, **NATURALISTIC** content within eudaimonia implies that I will have a criterion for ranking those goods, such as honesty and loyalty, in some order, so that when there is an apparent conflict I know which one I will choose.

Right judgement (phronesis) will cause me to choose to lie to save my friend, even if, as a virtuous person, I won't feel very happy about doing this because it "goes against the grain" of my belief in the virtue of honesty. I will do so because, in a flourishing life, friendship comes higher in the scale of goodness than not lying to my headteacher in this rather minor situation. Suppose the situation had been more serious (another judgement I would need to make using phronesis). For example, had I just seen my friend dealing cannabis to a student, phronesis would very likely take an opposite judgement - it was necessary in this case to tell the truth because the wrong action of drug-dealing was sufficiently serious to warrant my compromising the virtue of friendship.

So the virtue ethicist's response to Rachels is twofold. First, the role of rules in virtue ethics is as guidelines to facilitate decisions. They cannot be absolute categoricals as in Kantian ethics. Second, the wise person will know, by exercising right judgement, how to rank virtues in different situations. This does give virtue ethics a **RELATIVISTIC** element, at least in one sense of relativism. Goodness will always be relative to circumstances because we will need to identify the morally significant features of a circumstance before we apply the virtues, and those morally relevant features will not necessarily be the same in each case.

GILBERT HARMAN AND UNSTABLE CHARACTERS

Gilbert Harman, in a paper published in 2002, quotes the social psychologist Ziva Kunda with approval:

> *There is surprisingly little consistency in people's friendliness, honesty, or any other personality trait from one situation to another. We often fail to realise this, and tend to assume that behaviour is far more consistent and predictable than it really is. As a result, when we observe people's behaviour, we jump to conclusions about their underlying personality far too readily and have much more confidence than we should in our ability to predict their behaviour in other settings. (Kunda, Social Cognition, 1999:395)*

Virtue ethics grounds values in stable character traits or dispositions which become "second nature". But suppose there are no such stable dispositions, that human beings can be manipulated in different situations to exhibit whatever trait you wish to produce. Does this not undermine a central feature of virtue ethics, that by training and reflection we can develop a "second nature" which operates as a kind of moral reflex, so that we judge rightly how we should act?

Harman continues approvingly with his own analysis.

> *Having once attributed a trait to a given person, an observer has a strong tendency to continue to attribute that trait to the person even in the face of considerable disconfirming evidence, a tendency psychologists sometimes call "confirmation bias", a bias toward noting evidence that is in accord with one's hypothesis and toward disregarding evidence against it. (2002:3)*

Harman is arguing here that we tend to attribute stable character traits to people even when the evidence works in the opposite direction. The only way to come to a sound conclusion as to the stability of character is to perform an experiment where we have control groups with certain supposed characteristics and then observe whether their behaviour matches those characteristics. This is the purpose of the Seminary experiment discussed on the chapter on Christian Virtue Ethics and also of the notorious **MILGRAM** experiment in 1962.

Milgram advertised for a group of people to help with an experiment allegedly to discover how memory works. The idea was to place someone behind a screen and administer electric shocks when they got a simple answer wrong, in order to discover whether such punishments improved their ability to remember. In actual fact, the experiment was to determine how many of the participants would follow the directions of an authority figure in a white coat standing next to them who repeated the directive to any who showed hesitation: "it is essential for the experiment that you continue."

Milgram's findings were startling. Of those participating, 66% administered electric shocks to the person behind the screen of sufficient intensity to render them unconscious or even kill them. Only one third refused to go further when urged to do so when it was clear the subject was in distress.

Does this, asks Harman, show that people are generally evil?

> *What they show is that aspects of a particular situation can be important to how a person acts in ways that ordinary people do not normally appreciate, leading them to attribute certain distinctive actions to an agent's distinctive character rather than to subtle aspects of the situation. In particular, observers of some of the events that occur in these experiments are strongly inclined to blame those participants who did not stop to help or who provided intense shocks, thinking that the explanation of these agents' immoral actions lies in their terrible character. But the observers are wrong: that cannot be the explanation. (2002:5)*

Harman then proceeds to agree with Ziva Kunda when she argues that this is evidence not of no character traits at all, but that they are unstable. People react very differently according to the situation - extrovert in one setting, introvert in another, brave here and cowardly somewhere else. "Even slight variations in the features of a situation," concludes Kunda, "can lead to dramatic shifts in people's behaviour." (1999:499) Harman's conclusion is that the virtues can only work as predictors of behaviour where they are constantly reinforced by society or peer group.

Mark Alfano argues that we should distinguish between "high-fidelity" and "low-fidelity" virtues.

> *A high-fidelity virtue requires near-perfect consistency, whereas a low-fidelity virtue requires much higher consistency than one would expect without the trait in question. The high-fidelity virtues include chastity, fairness, fidelity, honesty, justice, and trustworthiness. If someone acts in accordance with chastity in 80 percent of the opportunities he has for cheating on his spouse, that hardly makes him chaste. If someone doesn't steal in 70 percent of the cases where she could, that doesn't make her honest. By contrast, low-fidelity virtues include charity, diligence, friendliness, generosity, industry, magnanimity, mercy, tact, and tenacity. (These lists aren't meant to be comprehensive or uncontroversial, but I hope they at least point in the right direction.) If someone gives to charity 20 percent of the time (assuming the sums are sufficient), that could count as charitable. If someone shows mercy even occasionally, that might qualify him as merciful. (Journal of Philosophical Research vol 38, 2013, p241).*

There is some mileage in this distinction, as it allows us to distinguish virtues (charity, mercy, fortitude) which don't have to be shown in every situation for a person to have those characteristics, from those which do seem to require absolute consistency (for example, chastity and faithfulness in sexual ethics). Applied to the Milgram experiment, it could be argued that "low-fidelity" virtues (such as mercy) failed to kick in because those involved were not sufficiently skilled in the virtue of **PHRONESIS** or right judgement.

Another answer to Harman's situationist objection is given by Christine Swanton (2003). She argues that in the Milgram experiment the participants were suffering from duress - acute moral pressure from the expert in the white coat. This again may show virtue that is not mature or reflective enough, but not the complete absence of virtue.

A third solution to the situationist claim of instability in the traits of character is to argue that virtues are radically contextual - something Alasdair MacIntyre argues by defining virtue as stable dispositions which occur within forms of life or "goods internal to practices." Because the practice of the Milgram experiment is somewhat odd (it has a deception at its heart), it is in itself not a good predictor of how people will behave in more stable and traditional forms of life, such as family, business, or sport, where the virtues and their context are clearer, more stable and better defined.

Put another way, given another chance, the Milgram participant who smiled sweetly and asked "is he dead?" would be unlikely to behave that way second time around.

ROBERT WACHBROIT AND THE ACCUSATION OF RELATIVISM

Robert Wachbroit writes of Alasdair MacIntyre's account of "practices", "plainly not every practice is justifiable and we might begin to wonder whether this crucial appeal to practices leads to **MORAL RELATIVISM**". (1996:110)

The word "relativism" is, however, ambiguous, having three meanings, and before discussing whether the charge is valid, it is important to clarify these.

Relativism can mean "goodness is relative to circumstances". It is in this sense, for example, that Joseph Fletcher calls situation ethics "principled relativism." Now, by this weak meaning of relativism, all forms of virtue ethics are relativistic, because a virtue only entails good actions when it is applied by the person practised in **PHRONESIS** in particular circumstances. There can be no absolute rule about how to apply the virtues.

But relativism has two further meanings. It can mean "particular to a culture" as opposed to "universal", in the sense that Natural Law holds that the proper functions of human beings are universal because they are shared by everyone. And finally, relativism can mean "subjective" rather than objective, where subjective means "up to me" and objective "measurable by some shared standard of truth".

Now Aristotelian metaphysical biology, the view that human beings share the same soul which is divided between rational and non-rational elements, is a claim to objectivity. Aristotle's argument is that the essential nature of human beings is something universal. Philippa Foot follows Aristotle in this point when she argues "the grounding of a moral argument is ultimately in facts of human life". (2001:24)

But MacIntyre's virtue ethics takes a very different view. Recall that MacIntyre rejects both emotivism as a form of subjectivism, and the "Enlightenment project" and its claim to objective, value-neutral reason (for example, Kant's argument for some form of "pure reason" or objective neutrality). He concedes in After Virtue that he must renounce "the claims of objectivity and authority of the lost morality of the past".

(1997:21) In a preface to the third edition of After Virtue he puts the case starkly:

> *What historical enquiry discloses is the situatedness of all enquiry, the extent to which what are taken to be the standards of truth and of rational justification in the contexts of practice vary from one time and place to another. If one adds to that disclosure, as I have done, a denial that there are available to any rational agent whatsoever standards of truth and of rational justification such that appeal to them could be sufficient to resolve fundamental moral, scientific, or metaphysical disputes in a conclusive way, then it may seem that an accusation of relativism has been invited. (1993, iv)*

There is no way, argues MacIntyre, to resolve disputes between different traditions which in turn have within them different practices sustained and supported by virtues. Doesn't this make any attempt to claim some objective basis for rationality impossible? Julia Annas thinks so, she writes,

> *There is, MacIntyre claims, no such thing as the Post-Enlightenment notion of rational justification in terms of reason or reasons that would have force with all rational persons irrespective of their social context. (Annas, J - Macintyre on Traditions, Philosophy and Public Affairs, 18, 1998).*

However, in his later works MacIntyre argues consistently against the charge of relativism. His arguments seem to have two main points: first, that traditions compete with one another and so develop and that conflict causes them to amend their own views. And second, that the

Aristotelian tradition is "superior" and so has some claim to objective validity over and above other moral traditions.

> *Tradition-constituted standpoints confront one another not only as rival moral theories but also as projects for constructing rival moral narratives. Is there any way that one of these rivals might prevail over the others? One possible answer was supplied by Dante: that moral narrative prevails ... which is able to include its rivals within itself, not only to retell their stories as episodes within its own story, but to tell the story of the telling of their stories as such episodes. (Three Rival Versions pp 80-81)*

Stephen Lutz sides with MacIntyre in this debate. MacIntyre's virtue ethics is, in the end, not a form of relativism, he argues because:

> *It is not truth that is relative, but the method of arriving at the truth which changes according to traditions and develops within traditions. What we have is just "the best account so far". Tradition is not the arbiter of truth, it is merely the bearer of tools with which its bearers seek the truth and those tools are subject to improvement. (Stephen Lutz, Tradition, p 84).*

If we accept this argument, the conclusion is paradoxical, Alasdair MacIntyre can both reject the idea of neutral ways of arriving at objective moral truth and at the same time argue that the objective moral truth still lies out there to be discovered.

The Four Questions Revisited

In the first chapter we laid out four questions which any moral theory needs to answer. The first two questions, "How is goodness derived?" and "How is goodness applied to circumstances?" are analytical questions. They concern assumptions the theory makes, its worldview, its view of rationality and the process of reasoning.

The second two questions are evaluative. The first asks "Is this theory useful?" in the sense of "Is the theory realistic?" In a sense this question explores what Elizabeth Anscombe lays down as a challenge to all theories in her 1958 article - Is there a philosophy of human psychology that fits what we understand of human beings? For if a theory is unrealistic, if it doesn't chime with what we understand makes human beings tick, we might as well discard it.

Our final question is also evaluative. "Why should I be moral?" is a fundamental challenge to all moral theories. Why live by this theory and not be a selfish egoist, simply pursuing my own self-interest? Why not be a moral parasite, feeding off the goodness of others? Why care about other people at all?

We now attempt an answer for these three questions from the viewpoint of virtue ethics.

DERIVATION

Virtue ethics is a naturalistic theory in the teleological tradition of ethics. It is naturalistic because it claims that goodness comes from certain natural features of what it is to be human (Aristotelian metaphysics, echoed by Philippa Foot) or some natural features of how groups work (MacIntyre's "goods internal to practices").

However, what marks virtue ethics out from deontological theories or the teleology of the utilitarians is that it focuses, not on the action itself, but on the character of the moral agent. It is therefore **AGENT-CENTRED**.

So there are two ideas of "goodness" here - the good person and the good action. Virtue ethics derives goodness from character traits or habits of character that build the flourishing life. The good person precedes the good action. The telos or end is **EUDAIMONIA**. These habits are both personal and social. They are personal in that it is my life that is being built towards the goal of perfection (Aquinas) or human flourishing (Aristotle). And they are social because character is built in the context of a **POLIS** (city-state) in Aristotelian thought, or a dynamic, changing tradition in MacIntyre's sociological theory of the virtues. So virtues are both personal (think of wisdom) and at the same time directed towards other people (think of compassion, mercy or justice for example).

Like utilitarian ethics, virtue ethics has one supreme end or **TELOS**. This end is the one thing, argues Arisotle, which is intrinsically good or good-in-itself. Eudaimonia, the state of well-being or flourishing, cannot be reduced to a further end. Virtues are developed to fulfil this intrinsic goodness, to establish the flourishing life.

Of course, this idea of eudaimonia isn't stable or fixed. It develops as our understanding of what it means to be human develops, or our practices develop within a tradition in MacIntyre's analysis of virtues. Virtues also change as they are good only in so far as they establish eudaimonia. We have seen, for example, that Christians like Aquinas add on virtues that the Greeks never had (obedience, chastity, humility). And in the chapter on applying the virtues, we saw that Rosalind Hursthouse calls for two new virtues - wonder and respect for nature - to be inculcated in children.

Goodness is therefore derived from a concept of eudaimonia that exists as a changing idea of what makes human beings flourish. Yet it resides, not in actions, but in character traits that produce actions. Goodness is about virtues and evil is about vices.

A good action then becomes the action which a virtuous person would do. This explains that in this second meaning of "goodness", that of the "good action", **PHRONESIS** is the key intellectual virtue. In Aristotelian virtue ethics, it is the key because it unlocks the secret of how to control the non-rational side of the soul. Appetites and desires are brought under the control of reason by the practice and development of practical wisdom. Phronesis is the process of learning to reason excellently about moral choices.

And in MacIntyre's virtue ethics, practical wisdom defines good action within the social context of a "practice" which forms within a tradition. A "good ball" in cricket is one that is straight and threatens to take a wicket. A "good father" in the practice of family life is one who listens, who plays with his child but also disciplines where necessary. So goodness and "good action" is relative in this sense to the practice.

APPLYING THE GOOD

Once we have determined a good habit of character, is this easy to apply in situations? The virtue ethicist agrees with Aristotle that the moral life is difficult and challenging. It will take, to quote Barry Schwartz, moral will and moral skill. The moral will is determined by our vision of the good life - the ideal of eudaimonia towards which we move. The moral skill is determined by our skill at practical wisdom.

Barry Schwartz argues that virtue ethics is superior to deontological ethics in generating right action because it focuses on the character of the agent rather than the action itself. He gives the example of a hospital cleaner who was good at his job, not because he could mop floors skilfully, but because he knew when to ignore his supervisor's order to clean the waiting room, because someone in there was asleep. In other words, the virtuous person knows when a rule cannot apply and knows when to break a rule. The virtuous person, argues Professor Schwartz, is like the jazz musician who knows the notes but is always improvising. It is this way that we apply the virtues using the skill of **PHRONESIS**.

It is Aristotle who seems to have the clearest idea of how phronesis would work. He argues that phronesis judges the mean between two vices - the vice of deficiency and the vice of excess. So the wise person judges the right form of courage to use in a situation. Too much (excess) would be rashness. So Colonel H Jones, during the battle for Goose Green in the Falklands War of 1982, grabbed a machine gun and ran towards the Argentine position as the attack faltered. He died doing so. Although he was awarded the Victoria Cross, we might call this "rash courage", or unwise courage. It's not wise, in a flourishing regiment, for a commanding officer to get himself killed.

Aristotle's view of the Golden Mean arises out of his metaphysics. It is wisdom which regulates the non-rational side of the soul. So temperance regulates the excesses of lust or greed. Wisdom knows which virtue is appropriate but also how it should be applied. Students often have problems in seeing how this would work, but the challenge is this: phronesis doesn't work in the abstract. We need a practical situation to illustrate how practical wisdom might generate the action that builds towards eudaimonia. We need to imagine an example.

The argument of virtue ethics is that, rather than being poor at guiding actions, it is actually superior to rule-based and other theories because it contains the sort of flexible judgement at its very heart which allows other virtues (compassion for the sleeping visitor in the example above) to bring about completeness. There is a unity in the virtues, argued Aristotle and Aquinas; only when they interact in this way (wisdom with compassion, wisdom with justice, wisdom with temperance) do we build the flourishing life.

REALISM

It is interesting that virtue ethics and the language of the virtues finds many echoes in modern psychology and the self-help manuals we find on the shelves of bookshops. So in business ethics we have Jim Covey's "Seven Habits of Highly Successful People". These are habits of character, or a store of wisdom which entail discipline. Habit 5 is "seek first to understand rather than be understood". Don't be an authoritarian dictator.

Moreover, cognitive behavioural psychology involves bringing the mind to bear in appropriate ways to understand and change behaviour. There are echoes of Aristotelian metaphysics here, as the rational side of the human psyche is brought to bear on the non-rational side.

Aristotle also suggests, more controversially, as Gilbert Harman's situationist attack illustrates, that once I acquire the proper character traits, these dispositions are "firm and unchangeable". (NE, 1105b1) So, while the virtues are not themselves sufficient for moral behaviour, truly virtuous individuals will usually do what's right even under the most difficult circumstances. (NE, 1105a88-10) If, on the other hand, virtuous character traits were not stable predictors of moral behaviour as Aristotle and others suggest, virtues couldn't result in virtuous actions. To meet the charge of situationism, that character traits are in fact unstable, the virtue ethicist needs to provide empirical evidence otherwise, or alternatively, argue that experiments such as Milgram are a distortion because the results are generated from such bizarre circumstances. For example, Milgram relies on people believing that the actors concerned are not actors and that the experiment has a good scientific purpose (rather than the possible evil effect of electrocuting someone for a minor offence of misremembering something). Testing morality in an environment that has this deception and abuse of trust at its heart is hardly a "good" experiment.

Virtue ethics, then, rather than being unrealistic, seems to conform to trends in human psychology which suggest that character traits can be analysed, formed and if necessary re-formed first by new habits of thinking and second by right action. We are not imprisoned in a determinist hell produced by our childhood, but are on a journey of self-formation towards an ideal of what we could become. This, at least, is the claim that the student of virtue ethics must evaluate.

MOTIVATION

Why should I follow the path of character formation laid down by the virtue ethicist? Why should I care about others?

James Rachels argues that virtue ethics handles the problem of moral motivation better than other theories (1996). How can this be so?

Philippa Foot (following Aristotle) argues that virtue ethics encompasses the whole of life, and meets our deepest needs and concerns. It involves all those motives and concerns we have as rational human beings - concerns which are special to the human species as a reasoning animal. So our motive is this: do we want to function well or excellently? Do we wish, in a sense, to fulfil our destiny? Do we want to have the satisfaction, joy and pleasure of a fulfilled life? The key here is to recognise certain universal human needs.

> *Men and women need to be industrious and tenacious of purpose not only so as to be able to house, clothe and feed themselves, but also to pursue human ends having to do with love and friendship. They need the ability to form family ties, friendships and special relations with neighbours. They also need codes of conduct. And how could they have all these things without virtues such as loyalty, fairness, kindness and in certain circumstances obedience? (2001).*

For example, imagine we are in hospital. A friend visits because she is compassionate, judges that it is the right thing to do and wants to visit. This is more pleasing for us than if she comes purely because it is her duty. Is she not a kinder and more compassionate person if she wants to make our day better by visiting us, than if she comes because she ought to? Do these qualities not enrich our lives as social beings with special relationships? Dr Patti Gardner, who cites this example, concludes:

> *Virtue ethics's account of motivation surely sits well with human society in which we develop special bonds and alliances that encourage us to behave well out of friendship, love, and loyalty. It is these elements that bind communities together and it is the weakening of such commitments that are seen when communities begin to fragment. (Journal of Medical Ethics, 2003, vol 29 p 297)*

So the rationale for morality in virtue ethics becomes an appeal to self-interest: do I want to live in a world typified by these virtues or in some other world? Do I wish to flourish, and take pleasure and satisfaction from it? Do I want to be a successful (excellent) human being, living in the best society I can imagine? If so - go bring the future about. Practise the virtues.

Key Quotes

ELIZABETH ANSCOMBE

"It is not profitable for us at present to do moral philosophy; that should be laid aside until we have an adequate philosophy of psychology, in which we are conspicuously lacking."

"'Man' with the complete set of virtues is the 'norm', as 'man' with, eg, a complete set of teeth is a norm. But in this sense 'norm' has ceased to be roughly equivalent to 'law'."

JULIA ANNAS

"A virtue is a disposition to act, not an entity built within me."

"I have to improve myself. No teacher or book can do it for me."

"Working out the answer is complex, because it requires thinking about what matters in a situation and what bravery demands."

ARISTOTLE

"Every action and pursuit is thought to aim at some good, and for this reason the good has been declared to be that at which all things aim."

"Human good turns out to be activity of the soul in accordance with virtue."

"That moral virtue is a mean between two vices, the one involving excess, the other deficiency."

"To be happy takes a complete lifetime; for one swallow does not make a spring."

"With the presence of one virtue, phronesis, all the other virtues will follow."

AQUINAS

"As the intellect of necessity adheres to first principles, the will must of necessity adhere to the final end, which is happiness."

"Freedom is ordered to the inclinations of human nature and fully expressed in the virtues and gifts of grace."

"Love is the mother and the root of all the virtues, inasmuch as it is the form of them all."

AUGUSTINE

"In marriage, sexual intercourse for the purpose of conceiving children has no fault attached to it. But used to satisfy lust, even with a spouse, it is venial sin."

SARA CONLY

"The possession of a virtue provides an internal stimulus to action."

PHILIPPA FOOT

"Virtues are in general beneficial characteristics, and indeed ones that a human being needs to have, for his own sake and that of his fellows."

"Virtues are corrective, each one standing at a point at which there is some temptation to be resisted or deficiency of motivation made good."

ROSALIND HURSTHOUSE

"These dispositions have to be inculcated from childhood in the moral training of character."

ROBERT LOUDEN

"If the primary moral question is not What is the right thing to do in a problematic situation? but What is a good life for a human being? morality suddenly seems to invade all corners of life."

ALASDAIR MACINTYRE

"I am born with a past; and to try and cut myself off from the past is to deform my present relationships."

"Virtue is an acquired human quality the possession and exercise of which tends to enable us to achieve those goods which are internal to practices and the lack of which effectively prevent us from achieving any such goods."

"The immediate outcome of the exercise of a virtue is a choice which issues in right action."

"The education of the passions is what ethics is all about."

"Virtues are dispositions to feel in certain ways."

"Human begins have a specific nature such that they move by nature towards a specific telos."

JEAN PORTER

"Rationality is tradition-guided enquiry."

TOM WRIGHT

"In order to develop Christian character the first step is suffering."

KEY TERMS

- **ARETE**
- **EMOTIVISM**
- **ERGON**
- **EUDAIMONIA**
- **FORM OF LIFE**
- **FINAL CAUSE**
- **GOLDEN MEAN**
- **"GOODS INTERNAL TO PRACTICES"**
- **INSTRUMENTAL**
- **INTRINSIC**
- **NATURALISM**
- **PHRONESIS**
- **TELOS**
- **TELEOLOGICAL**
- **TRADITION**

SELF-TEST: KEY QUESTIONS

1. What is the best definition of a "virtue"?

2. Explain how virtues could be seen as "skills".

3. What is the importance of phronesis for virtue ethics?

4. Explain Aristotle's "metaphysical biology".

5. What elements of Aristotelian virtue ethics does MacIntyre reject?

6. What makes Philippa Foot's virtue ethics distinctive?

7. Is it correct to describe both Foot and MacIntyre as "Aristotelian"?

8. How can virtue ethics be applied to sexual ethics?

9. What new virtues does Hursthouse suggest to help protect the environment?

10. "Virtue ethics is a form of relativism." Discuss.

FURTHER READING

ANSCOMBE, GEM - (1958) Modern Moral Philosophy. (Philosophy 35)

AQUINAS, T - Summa Theologica. (New Advent)

ARISTOTLE - (1926) Nichomachean Ethics, Harvard University Press.

FOOT, P - (2001) Natural Goodness, Oxford University Press

FOOT, P - (2002) Virtues and Vices and other essays in Moral Philosophy, Oxford University Press

GRABOWSKI, J - (2003) Sex and Virtue, Catholic University Press

HACKER-WRIGHT, J - (2013) Philippa Foot's Moral Thought, Bloomsbury

HURSTHOUSE, R - (1991) Virtue theory and Abortion, Philosophy & Public Affairs, Vol 20, no. 3, summer

HURSTHOUSE, R - Environmental Virtue Ethics. In Rebecca L Walker (Editor), Philip J Ivanhoe (Editor) (2009) Working Virtue: Virtue Ethics and Contemporary Moral Problems, Oxford University Press

KORNEGAY, R - (2011) Jo Hursthouse's Virtue Ethics and Abortion: Abortion ethics without metaphysics? (Ethical Theory and Moral Practice 14(1): 2011:51–71)

MACINTYRE, A - (1997 2nd Ed) After Virtue, Gerald Duckworth

RACHELS, J - (1993) The Elements of Moral Philosophy, McGraw-Hill, chapter 7

VAN HOOFT, S - (2006) - Understanding Virtue Ethics, Acumen Publishing.

WRIGHT, T - (2010) Virtue Reborn, SPCK, 2010